# Resting Places

An artistic collaboration intersecting
Remembrance, Nature,
Love and Death

*Photography by Mary T. Wagner*
*Paintings by Erico Ortiz*

Exhibition dates October 4 - 27, 2014

Inspiration Studios
1500 S. 73rd Street
West Allis, WI  53214

www.inspirationstudiosgallery.com

# Resting Places

Edited by Mary T. Wagner

Copyright October 1, 2014 Waterhorse Press LLC

Front cover photo "Simpson Farman" © Mary T. Wagner 2014
Back cover acrylic on wood "Keeping Watch Over Pueblo" © Erico Ortiz 2014

Visit Mary T. Wagner's website at

**www.marytwagner.com**

Visit Erico Ortiz's website at

**www.ericosgallery.blogspot.com**

ISBN-13: 978-0692285800
ISBN-10: 0692285806

# WATERHORSE PRESS

# Table of Contents

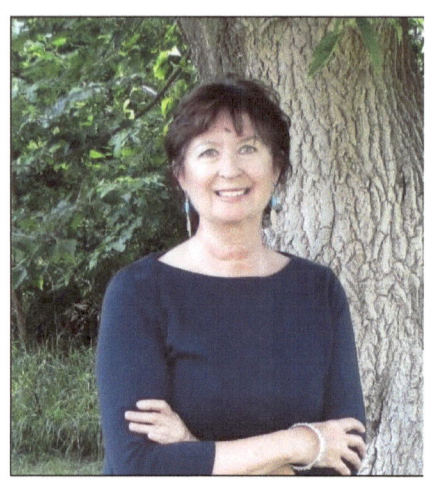

**MOST OF THE BEST THINGS** in my life have happened by chance or by accident, and hanging around rural graveyards taking photos is certainly one of them! I'm a writer, among many other things, and was working on a scene set in a small, neglected rural cemetery in a book I was writing. I decided that a visit to just such a place with my camera would allow me to both get a visceral sense of the place…and capture minute visual details I'd surely forget by the time I got back in the car.

I was utterly unprepared by how the place captured my imagination that foggy autumn day, or how I would find myself drawn again and again to these poignant places.

Whether ornate and well-maintained, off the beaten path on two-lane country roads, or beside steepled churches in small towns, the graveyards and their stone markers stand as testaments to the fact that we want to be remembered, and that we mattered, and that we were, above all, loved. I have come across some cemeteries that are so small that they are not even on the map. Often the only sounds that I hear are crickets chirping and birds warbling, a dog's far-off bark, the whinny of a horse in a pasture nearby, the wind in nearby branches.

And in the places that are more forgotten and less visited than others, there is a strange peace and beauty—the fragrant crush of wild mint underfoot or the smell of lilacs nearby, the blaze of white trilliums and purple violets among the stones, a swirl of dead oak leaves from the winter before, resting against worn marble, brown and curled like scraps of leather. As my fingers trace the worn letters, I know that here was love.

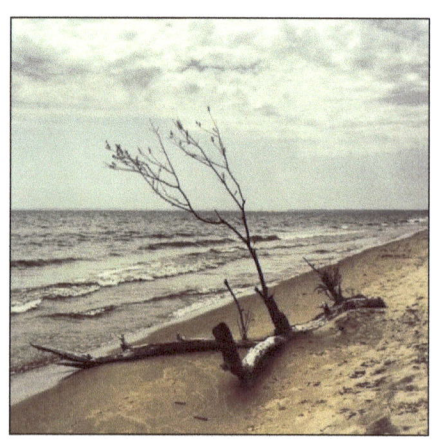

*Mary T. Wagner*

Driftwood, Reborn *2014*

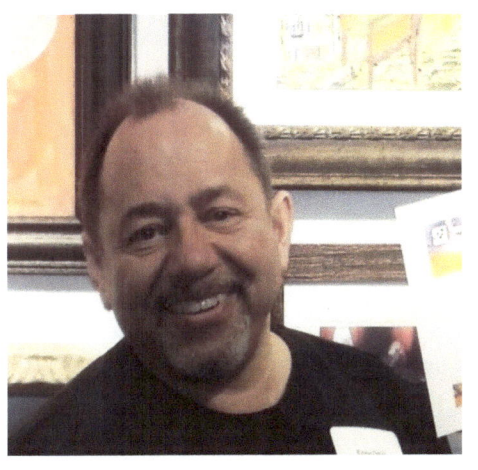

In 1998, a study leave immersed me in art education courses. While this was not the traditional studio coursework that a budding artist would undertake, I learned the value of critical thinking and problem-solving as they relate to educating students in the arts, a great bit of knowledge for a school administrator looking to support his educators. After years of rather humble artistic endeavors at home and in the community, my retirement from the Milwaukee Public Schools in 2011 provided the opportunity I needed to explore visual arts as never before. I began to paint! I realized that inspiration was all around me—in people and places, sights and sounds, music and movies.

As part of my creative process, I determine the idea for a project. Then comes the challenge of selecting, mixing, and blending colors to achieve a certain effect on a canvas, a challenge I truly enjoy. Sometimes that selection process takes on a life of its own... and I'm forced to abandon my initial intention to give way to a new creative thought. Still honing skills and techniques, I am often thrilled (and sometimes pleasantly surprised!) by the resulting color compositions and the overall product.

Since beginning this new phase in my life, many doors have opened for me. What began as a hobby has become a lifelong passion, including the opening of Inspiration Studios in West Allis, where theatre and music and art can meet. The arts have become my way of viewing the world and expressing my mind's eye on stage and now on canvas. You will see through my paintings that I am still finding my way.

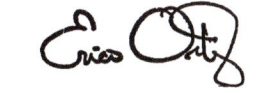

www.ericosgallery.blogspot.com
www.inspirationstudiosgallery.com

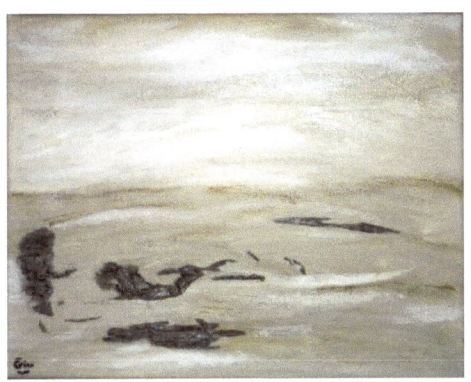

Sand Sculptures
*Acrylic, 2014*

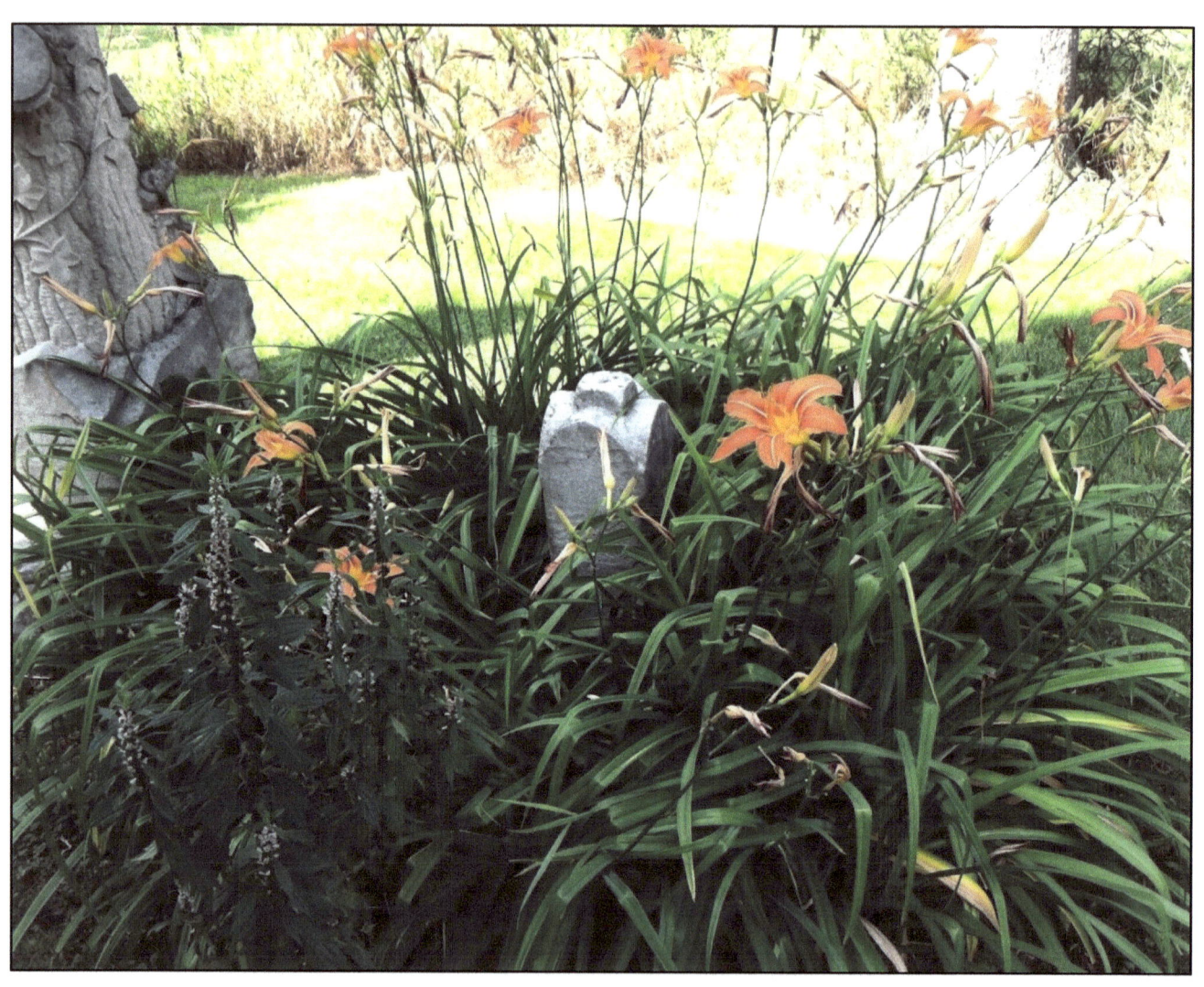

In the Lilies

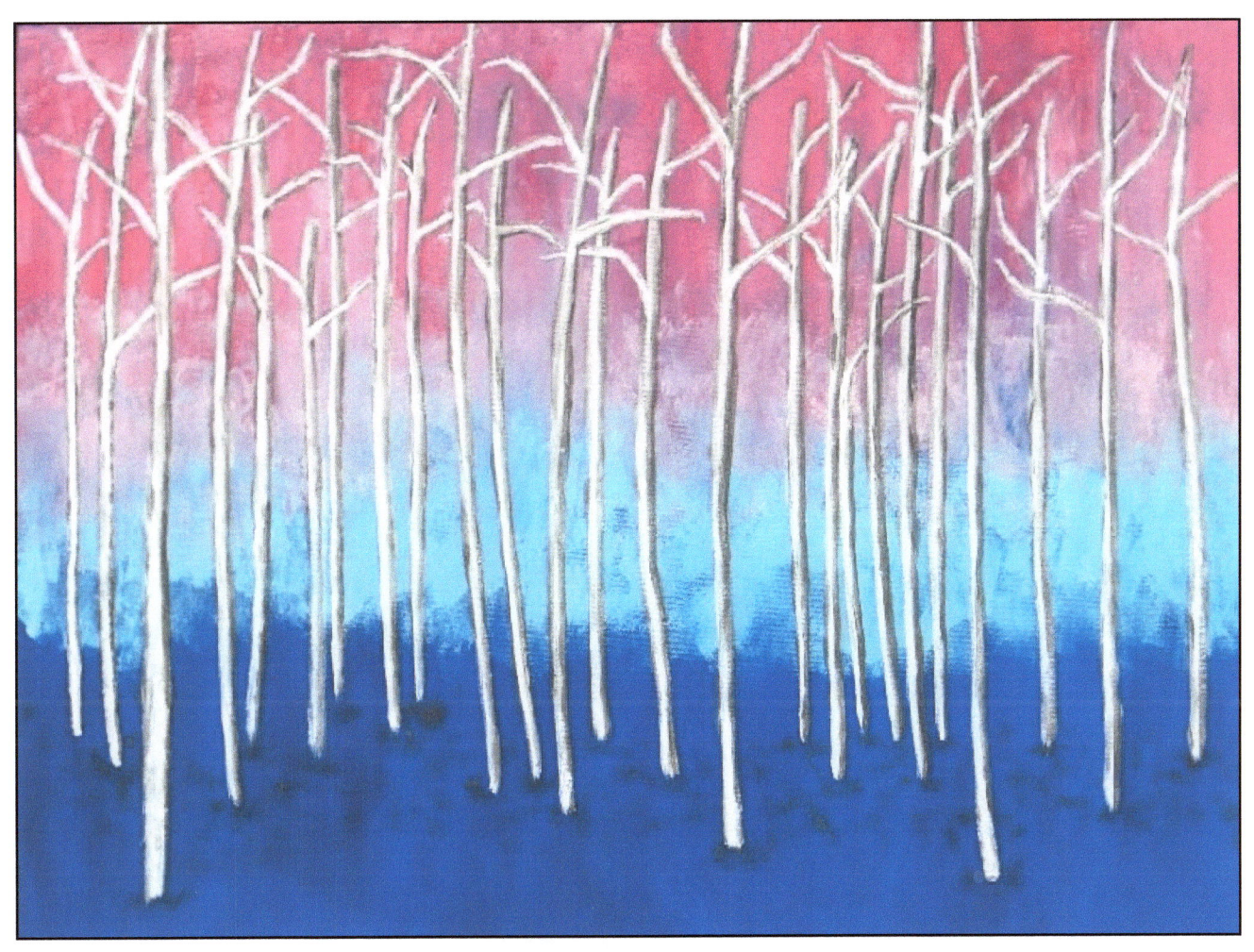

Pink Forest
*Acrylic, 2012*

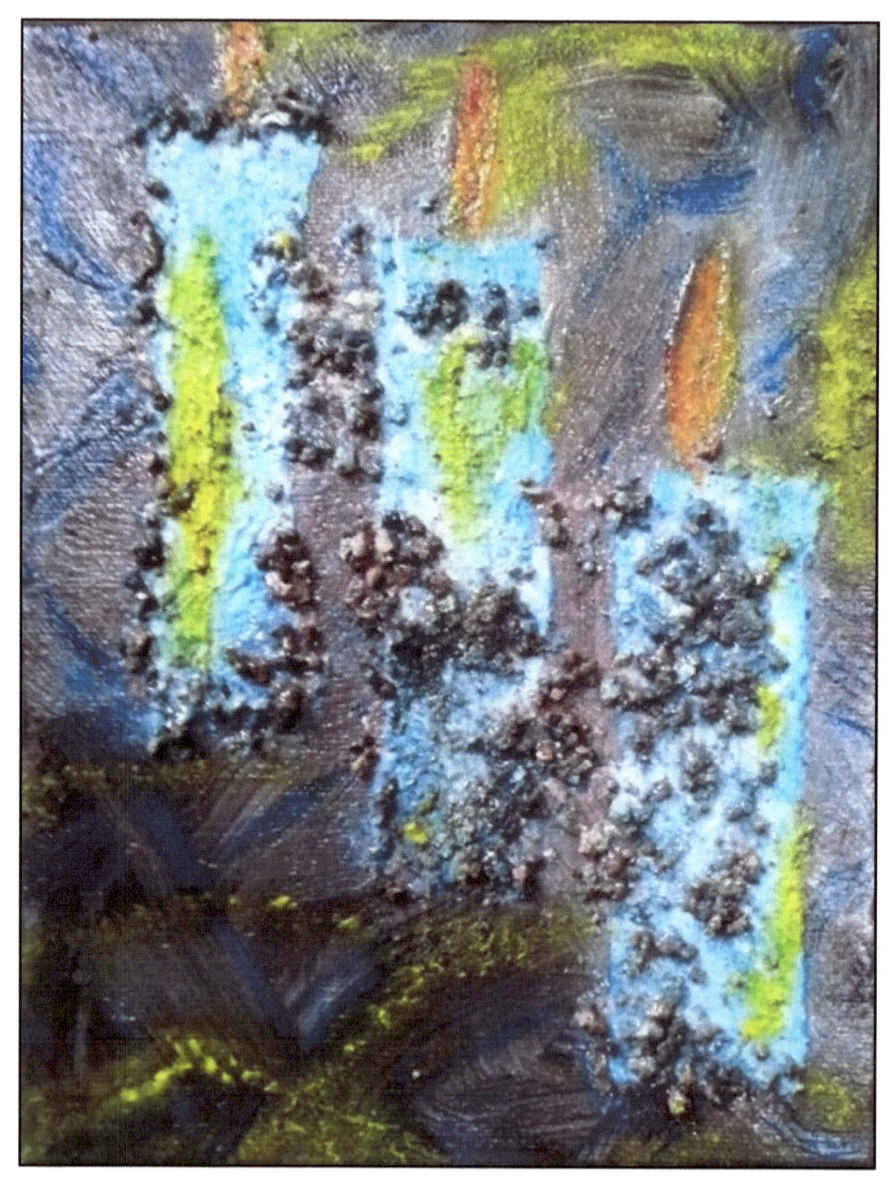

Velitas de Esperanza/Candles of Hope
*Mixed media, 2013*

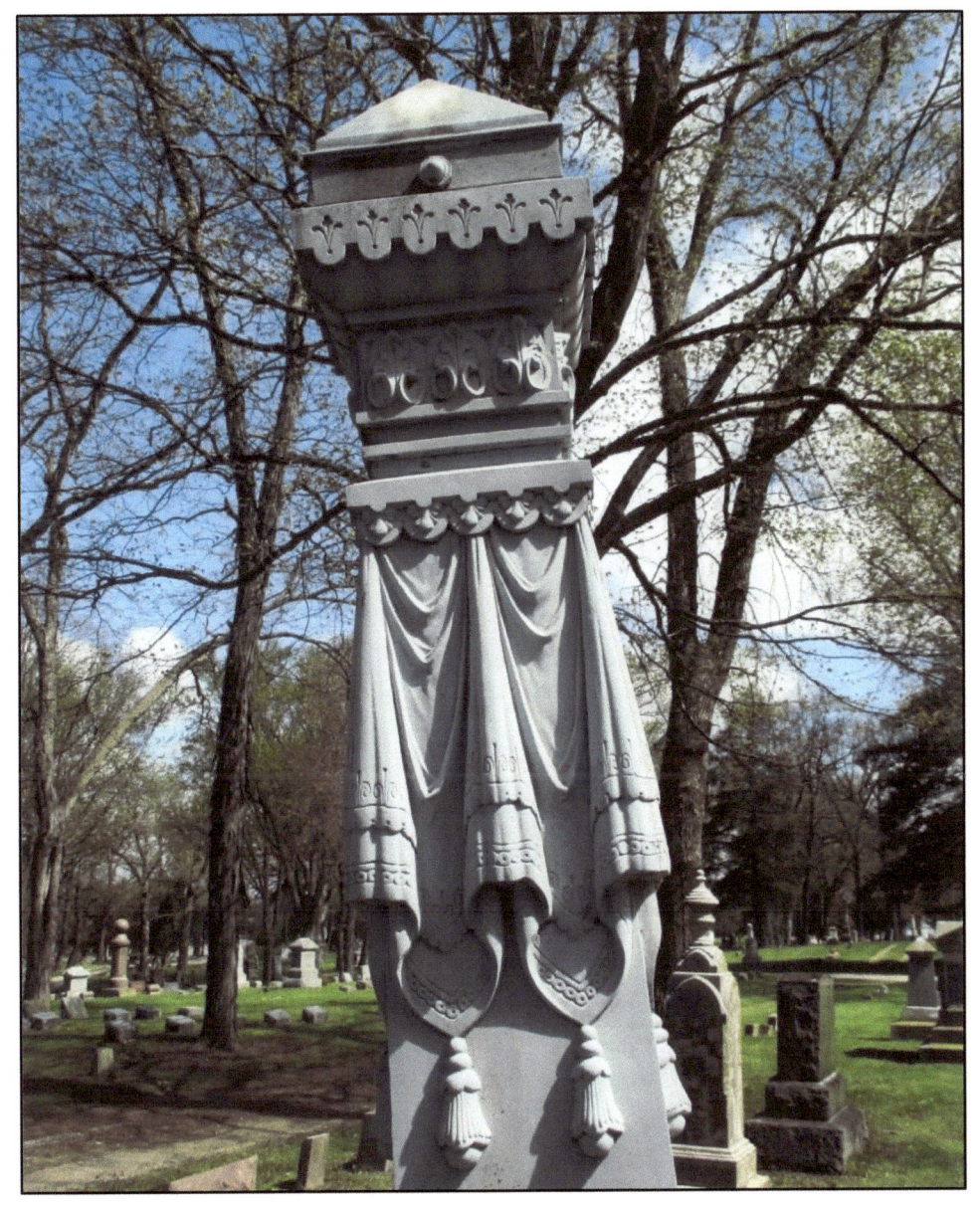

Adornment

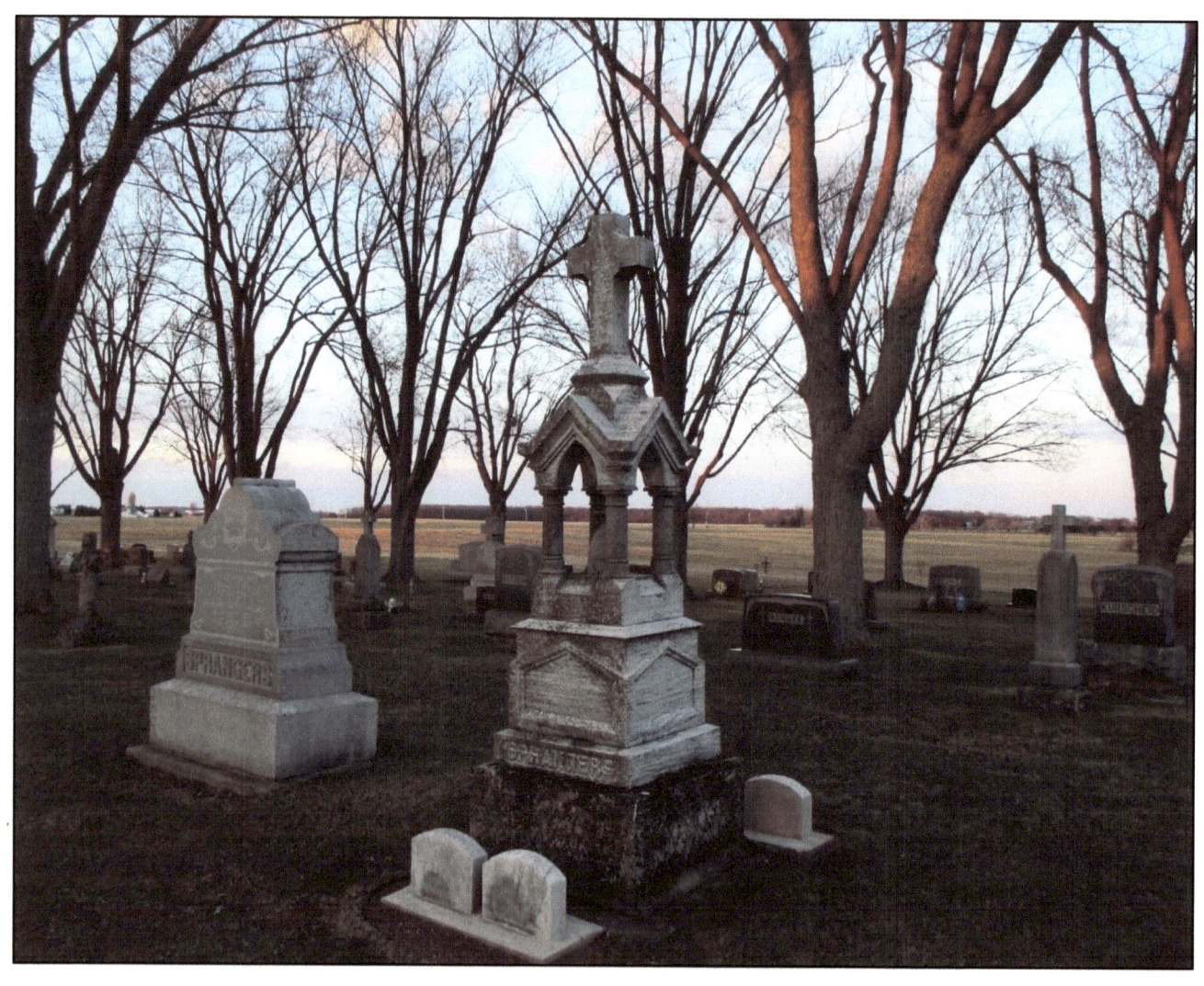

At Eventide

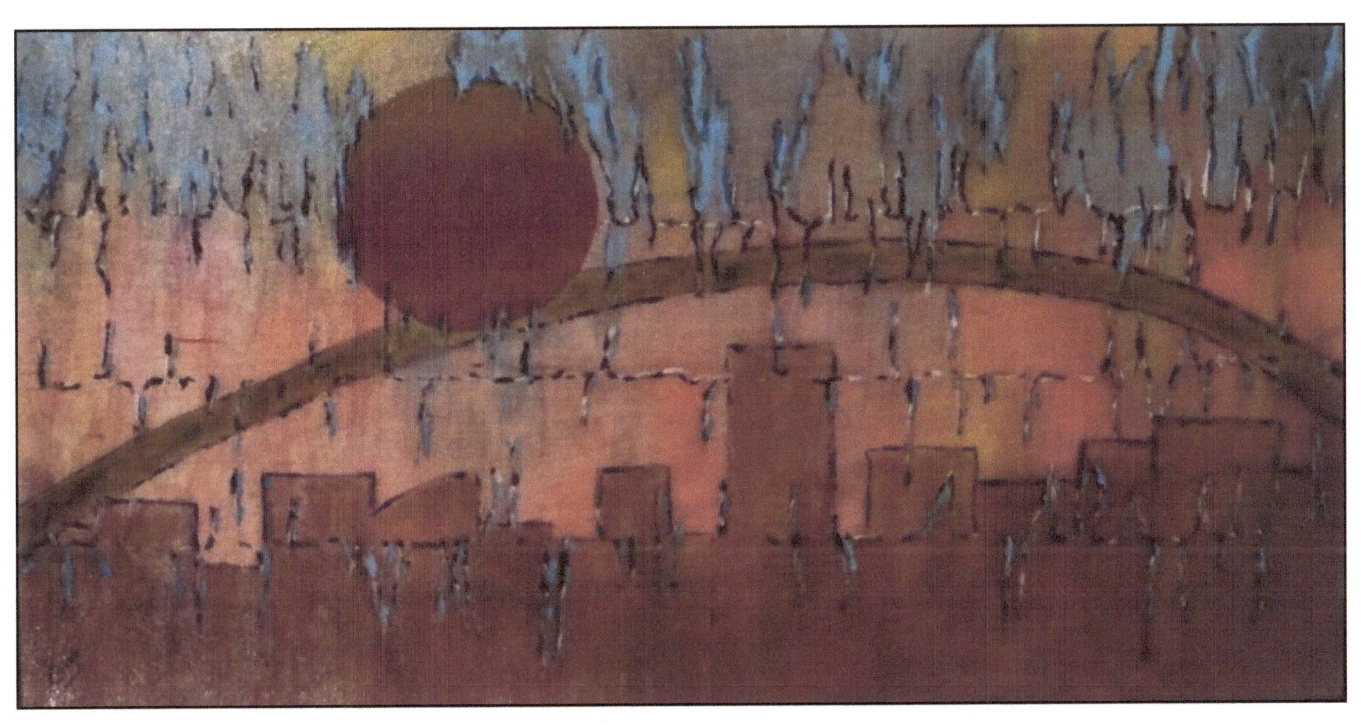

Skyline
*Watercolor on wood, 2014*

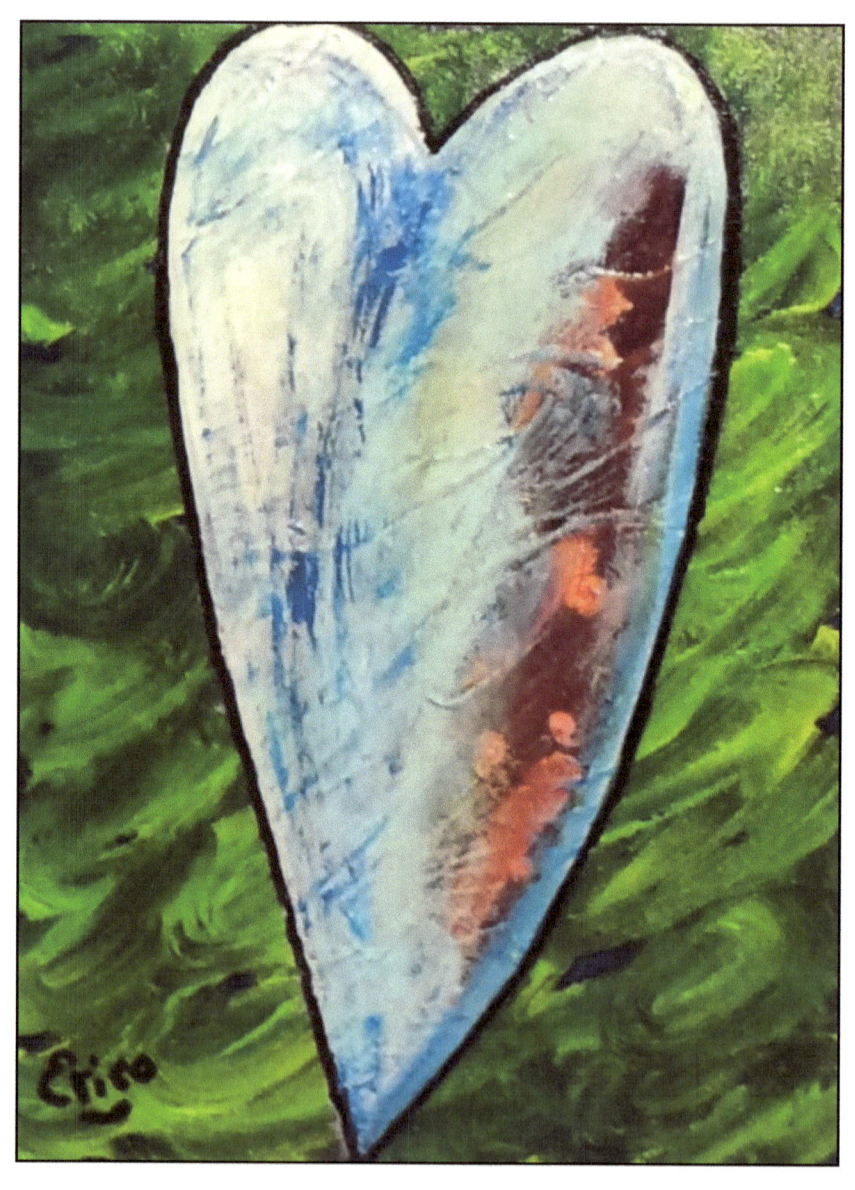

**Blue Heart**
*Acrylic on wood, 2013*

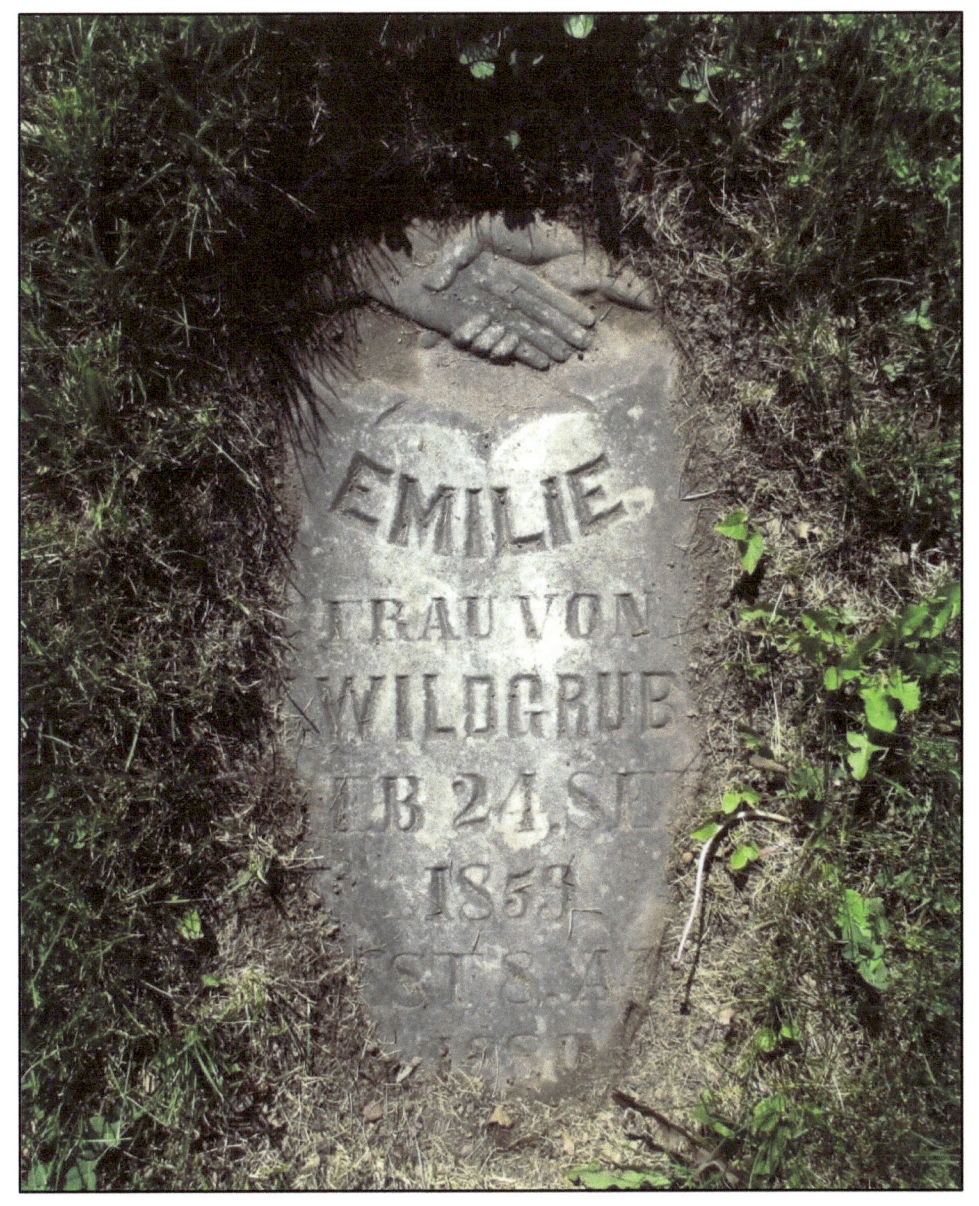

From Dust to Dust

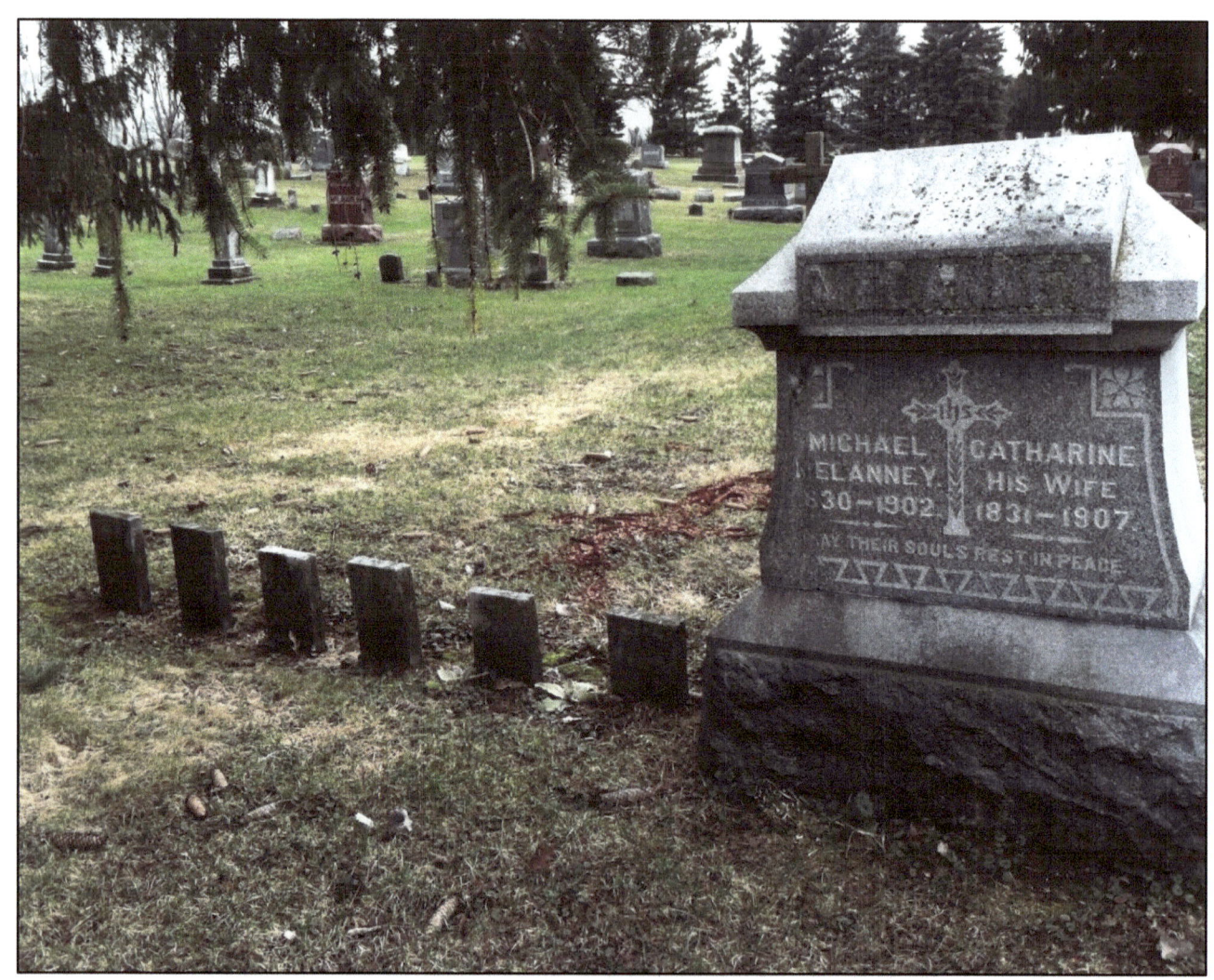

Family Line

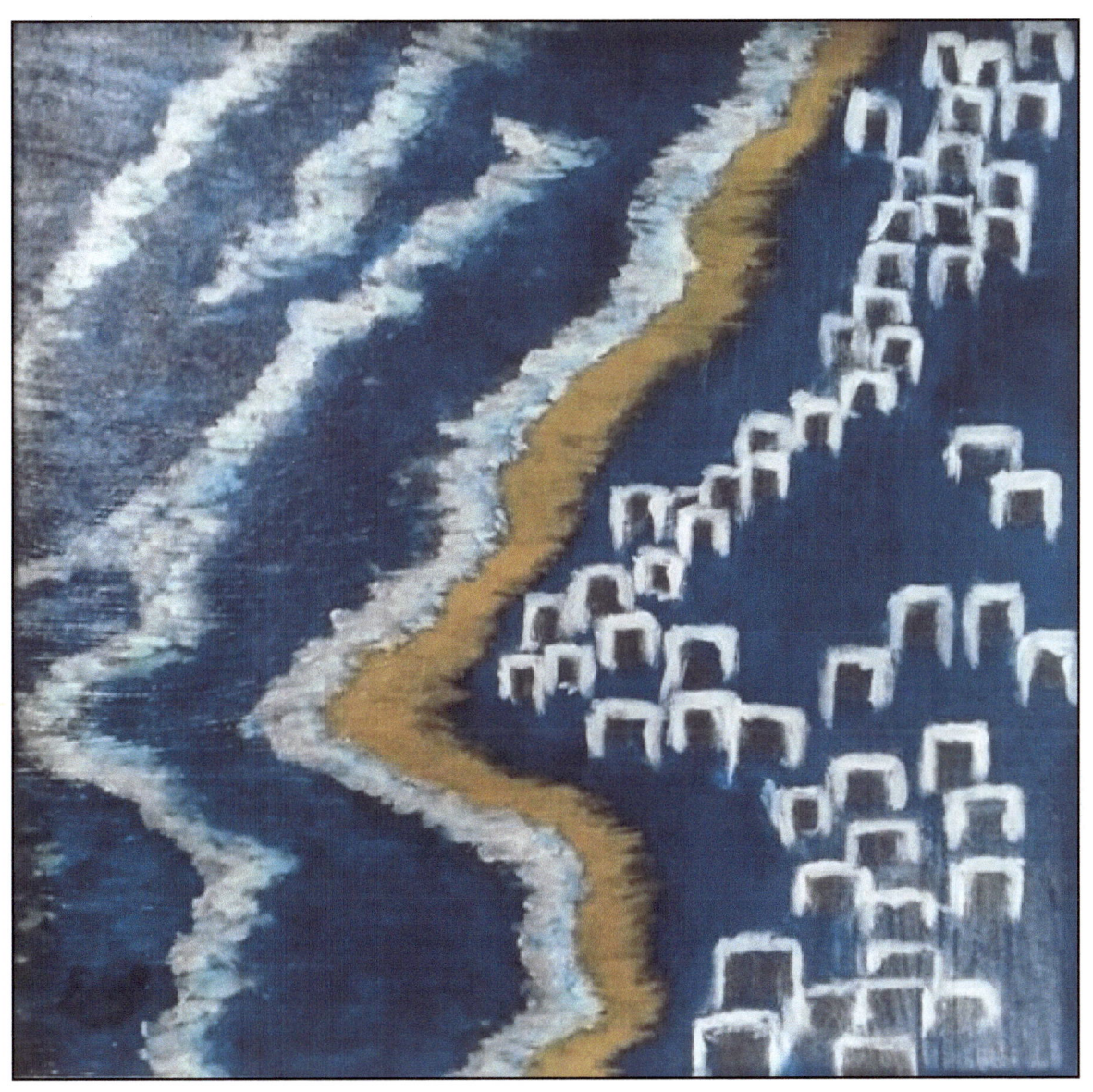

**Isla Blanca/White Island**
*Acrylic, 2013*

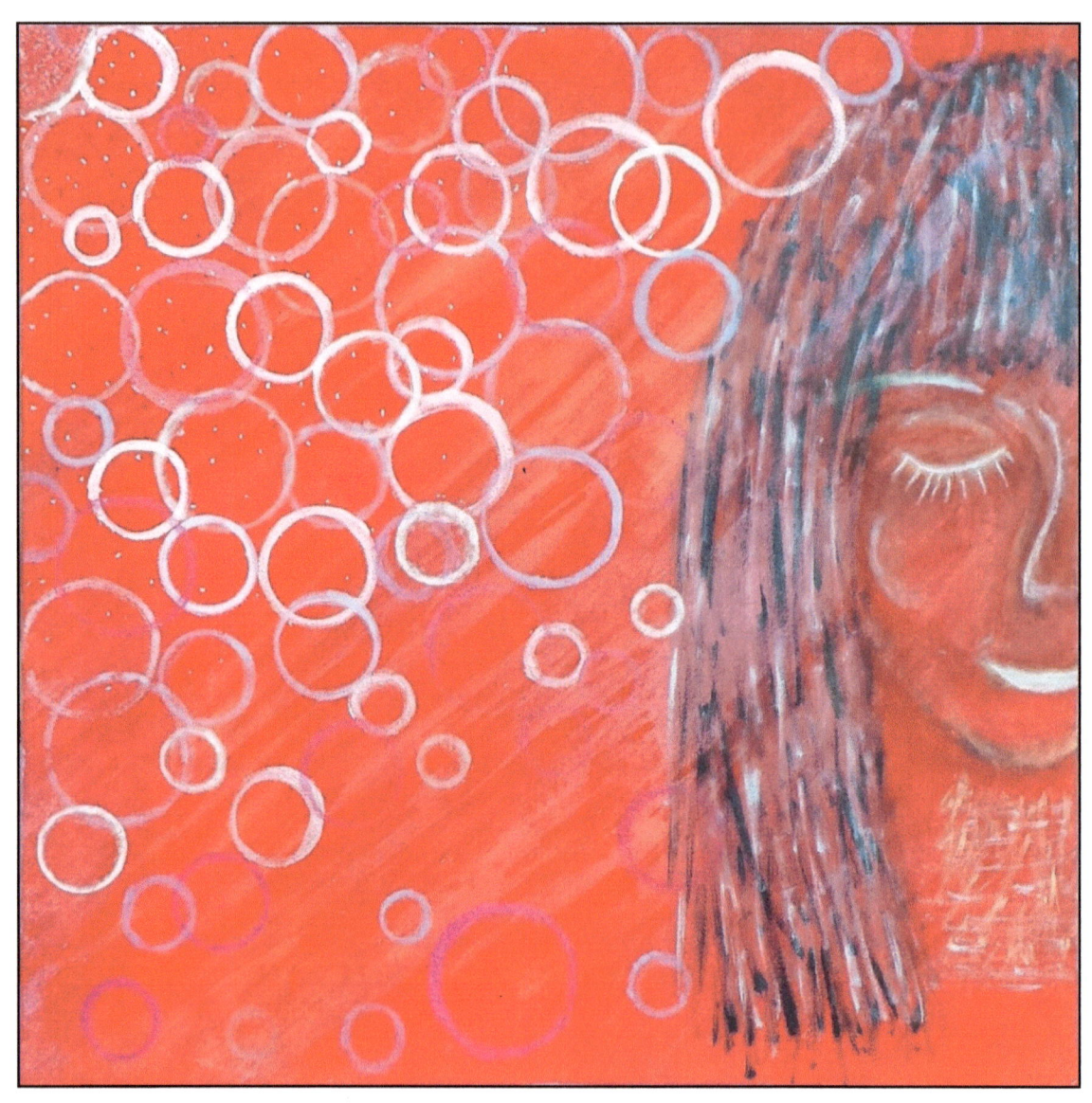

Star
*Acrylic, 2014*

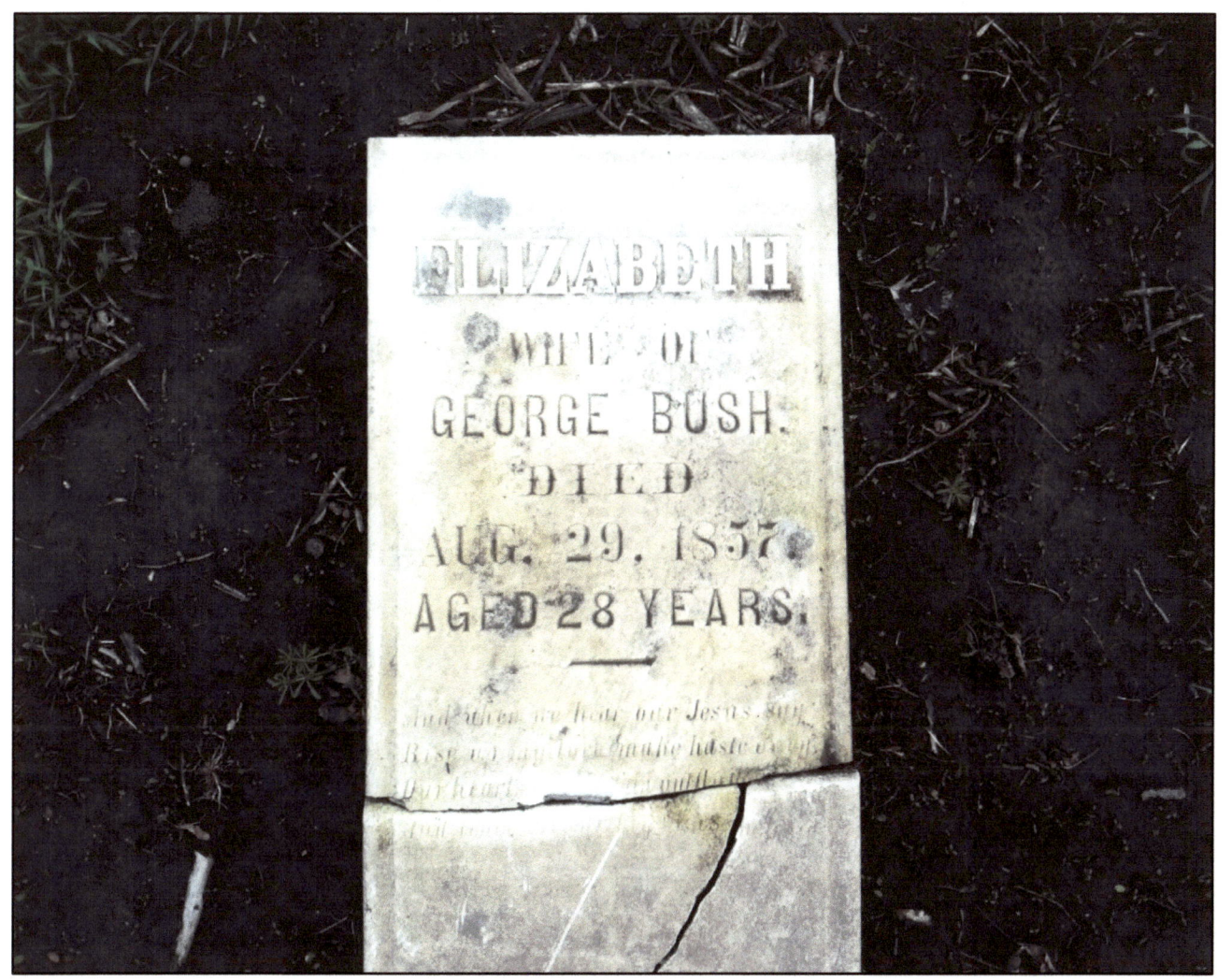

Elizabeth Bush

*And when we hear our Jesus say, rise up my love, make haste away!*
*Our hearts would fain outfly the wind and leave all earthly loves behind.*

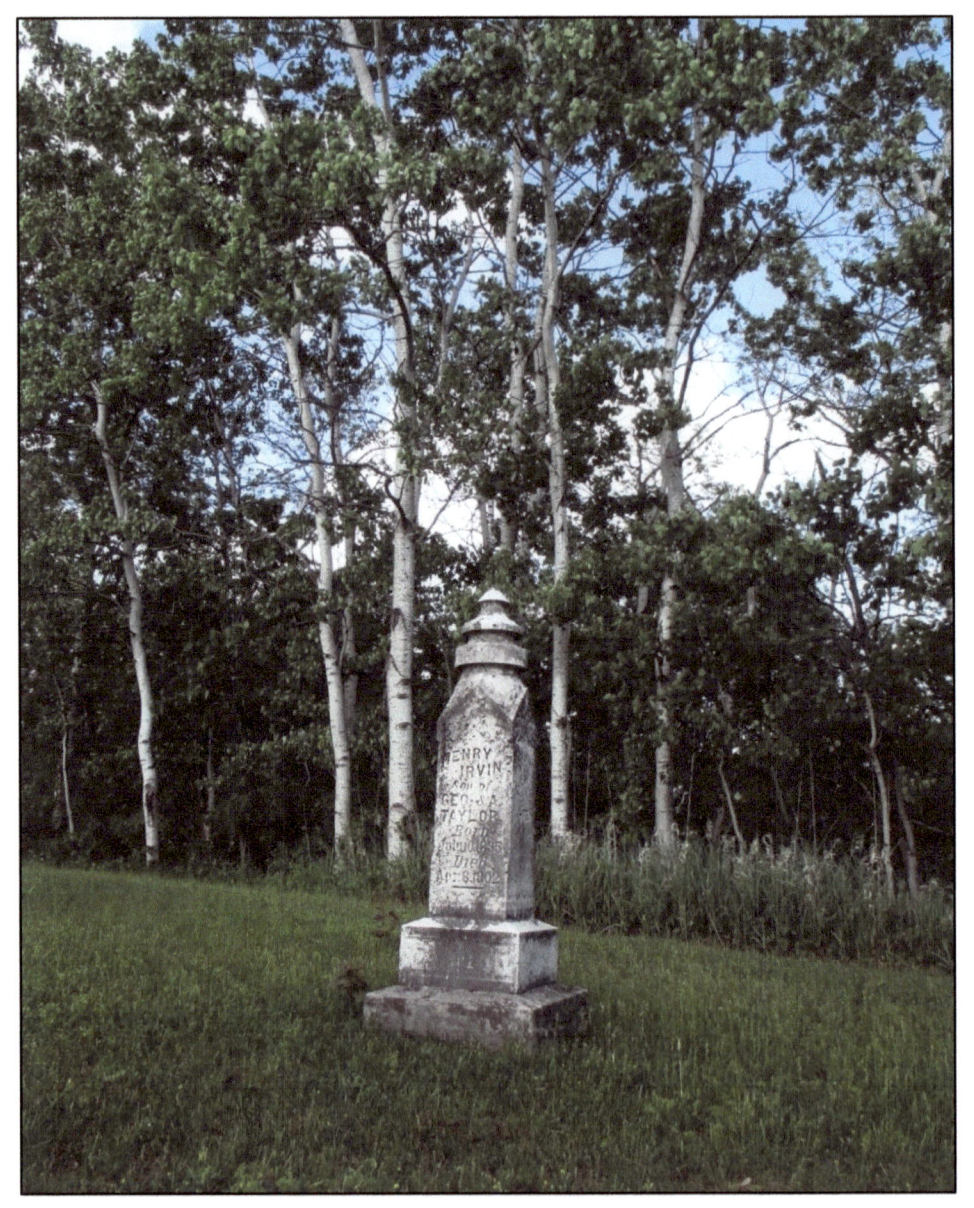

With Tall Companions

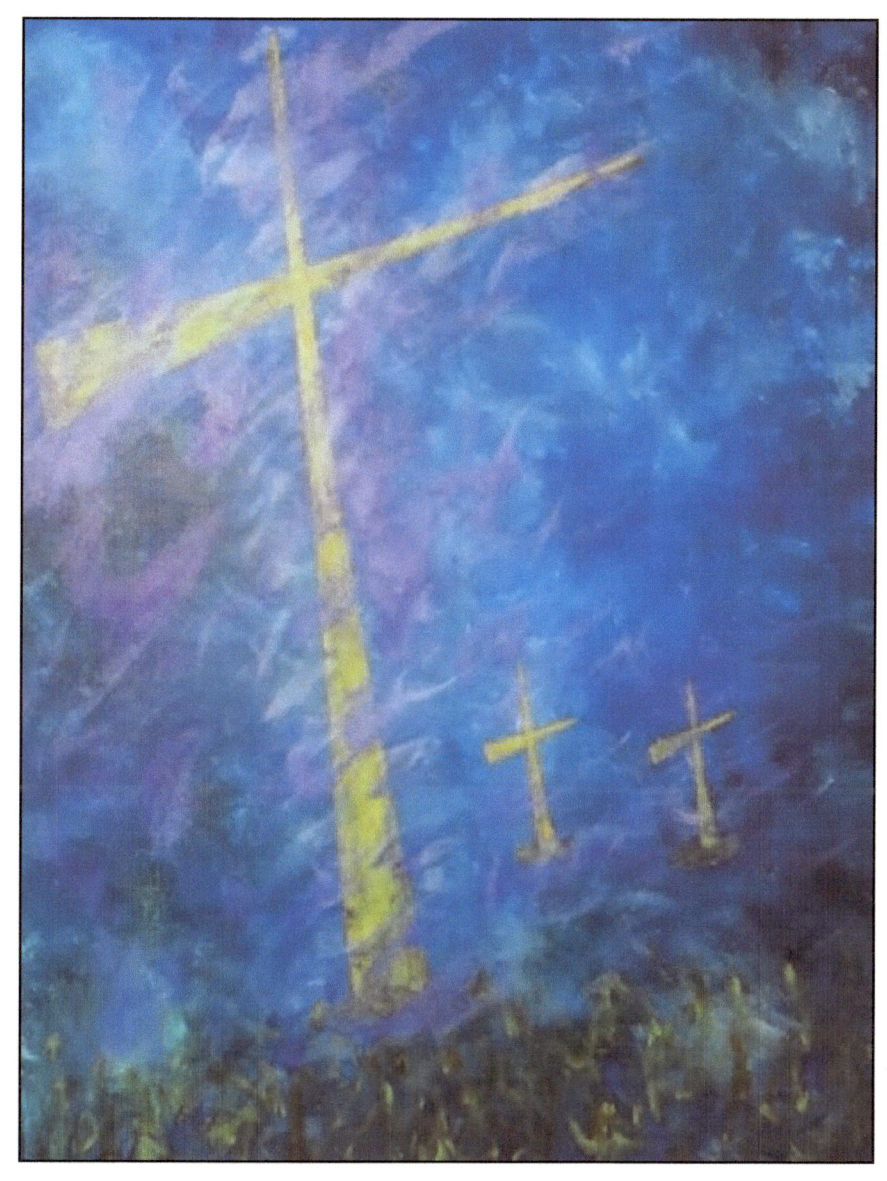

**Three Crosses**
*Acrylic, 2014*

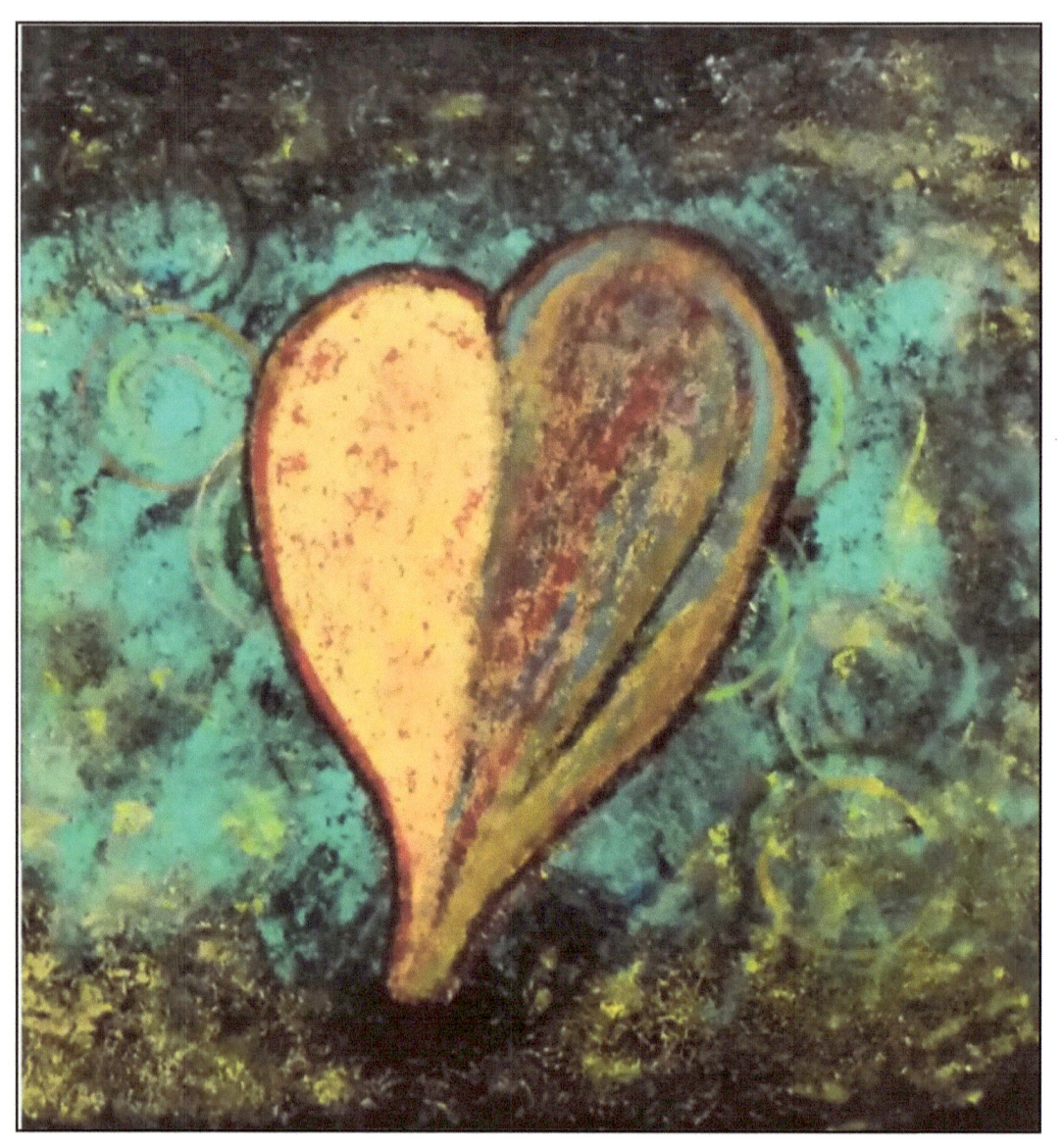

**Tainted Heart**
*Acrylic on wood, 2014*

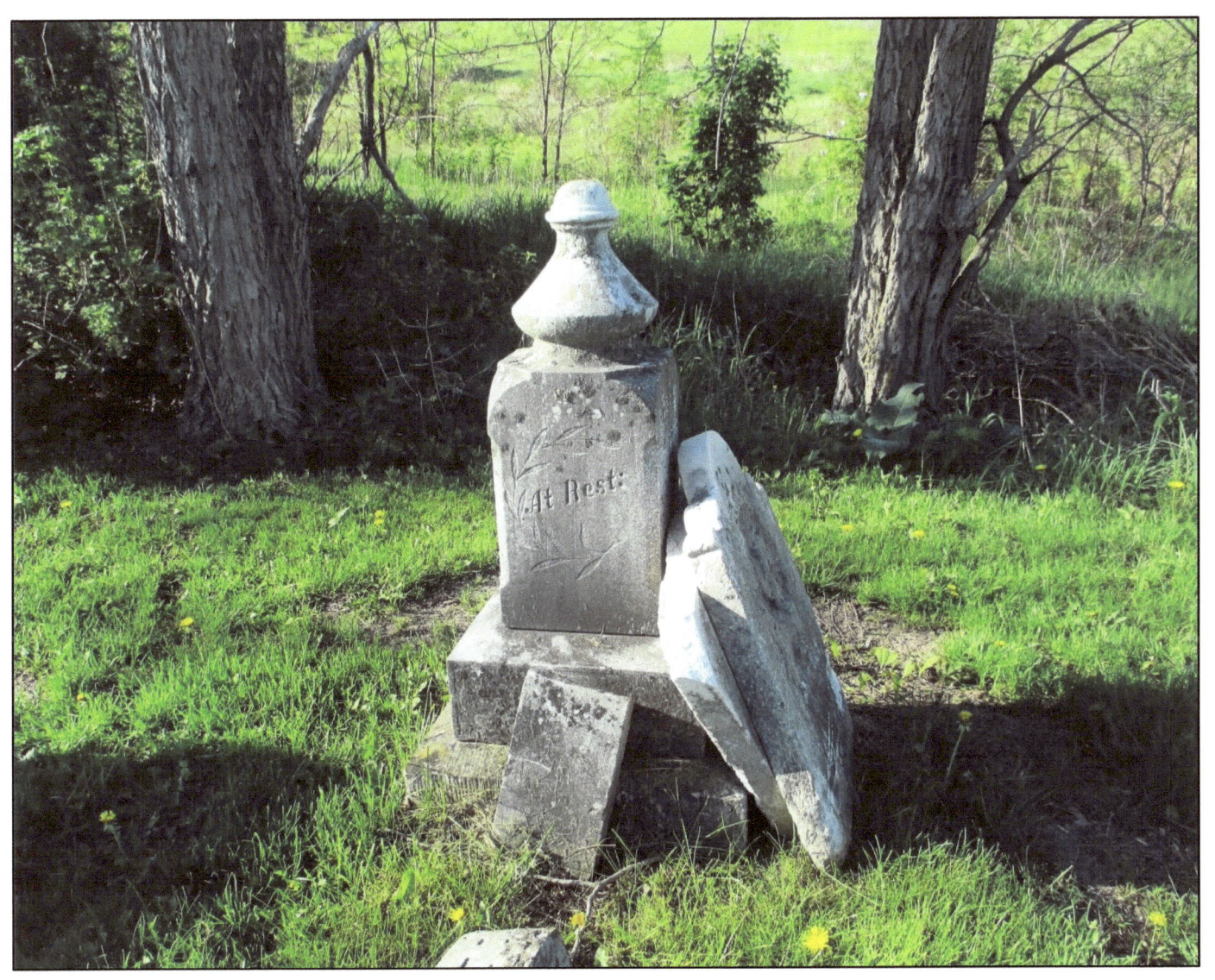

At Rest

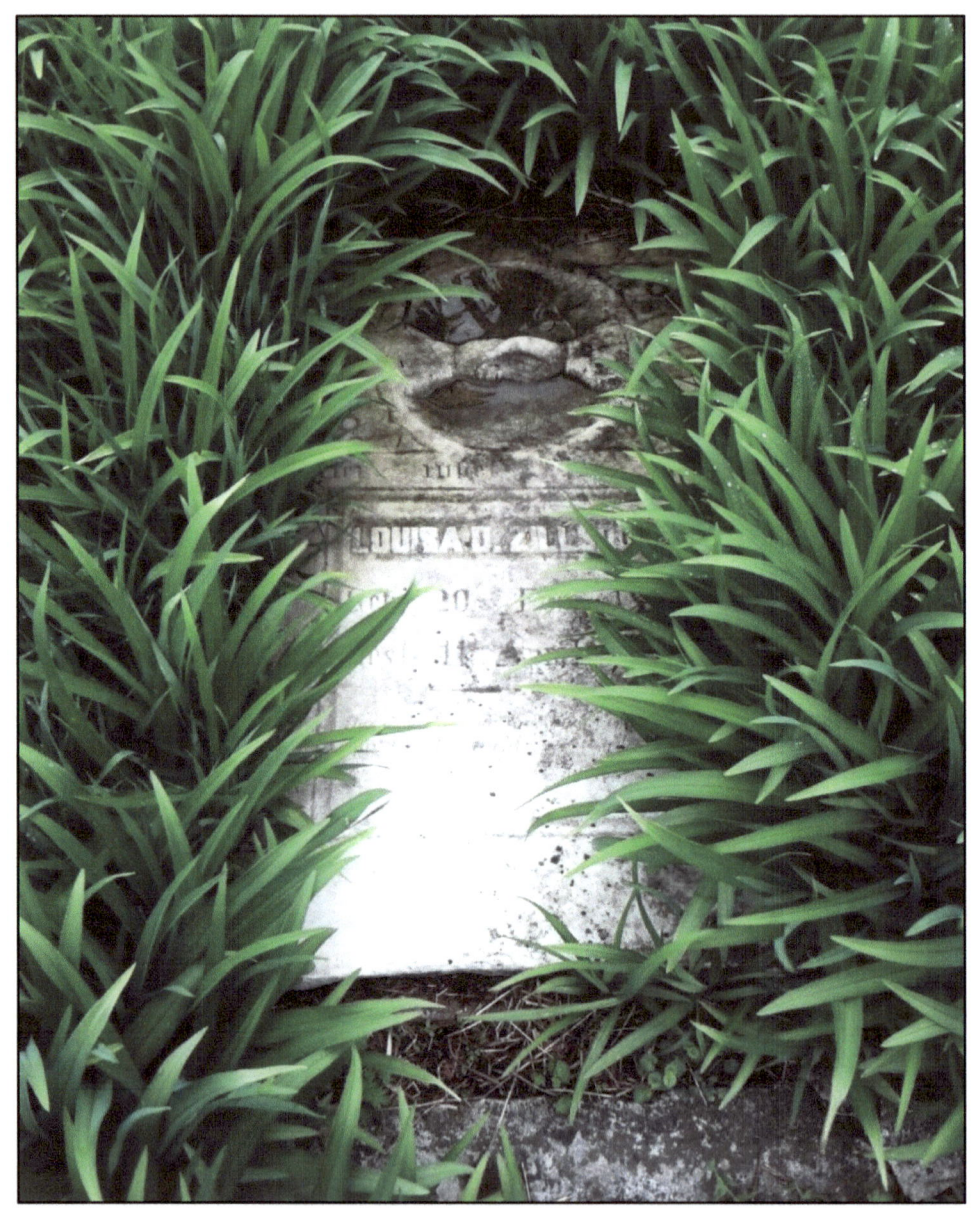

Enfolded

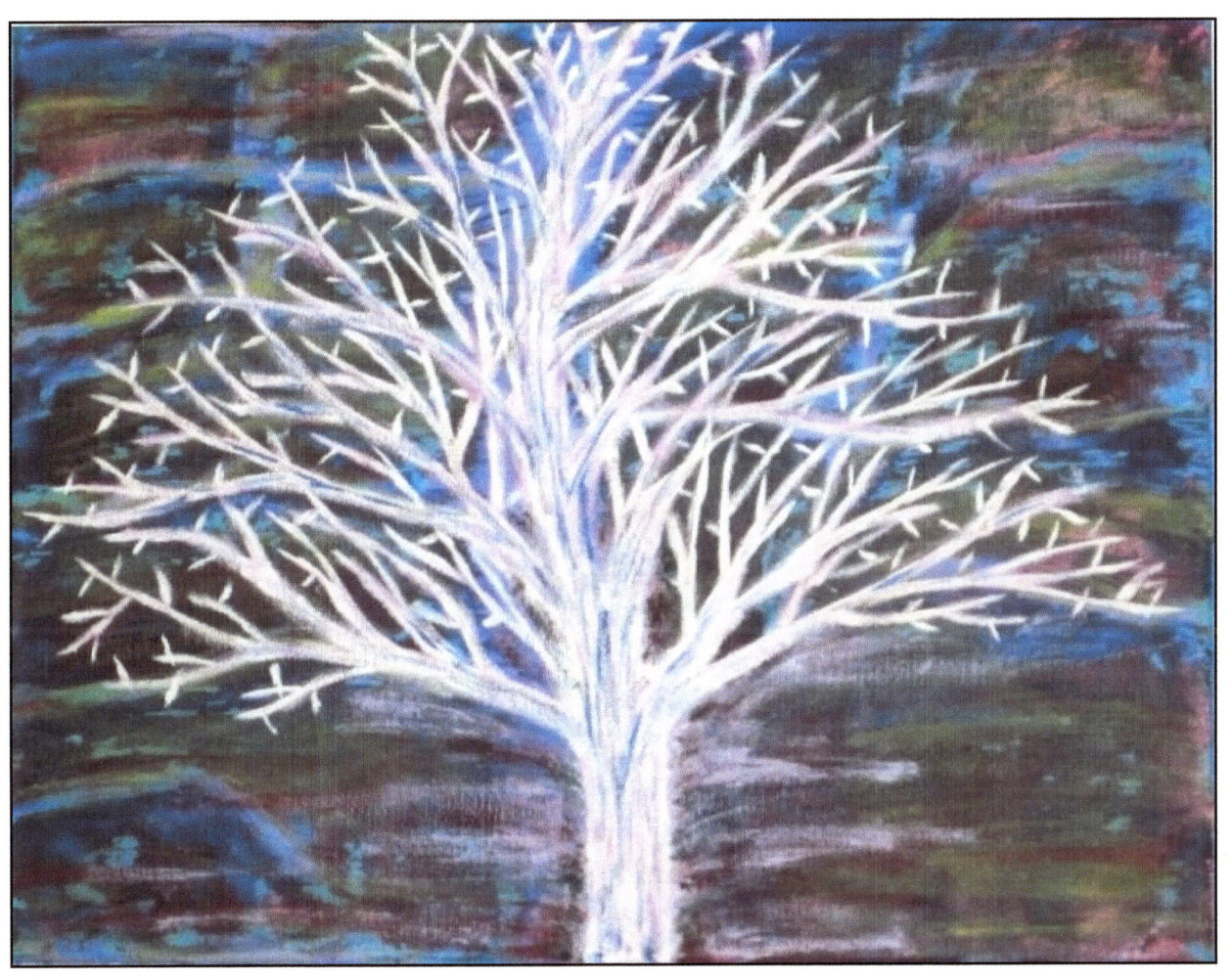

Solitude
*Acrylic, 2012*

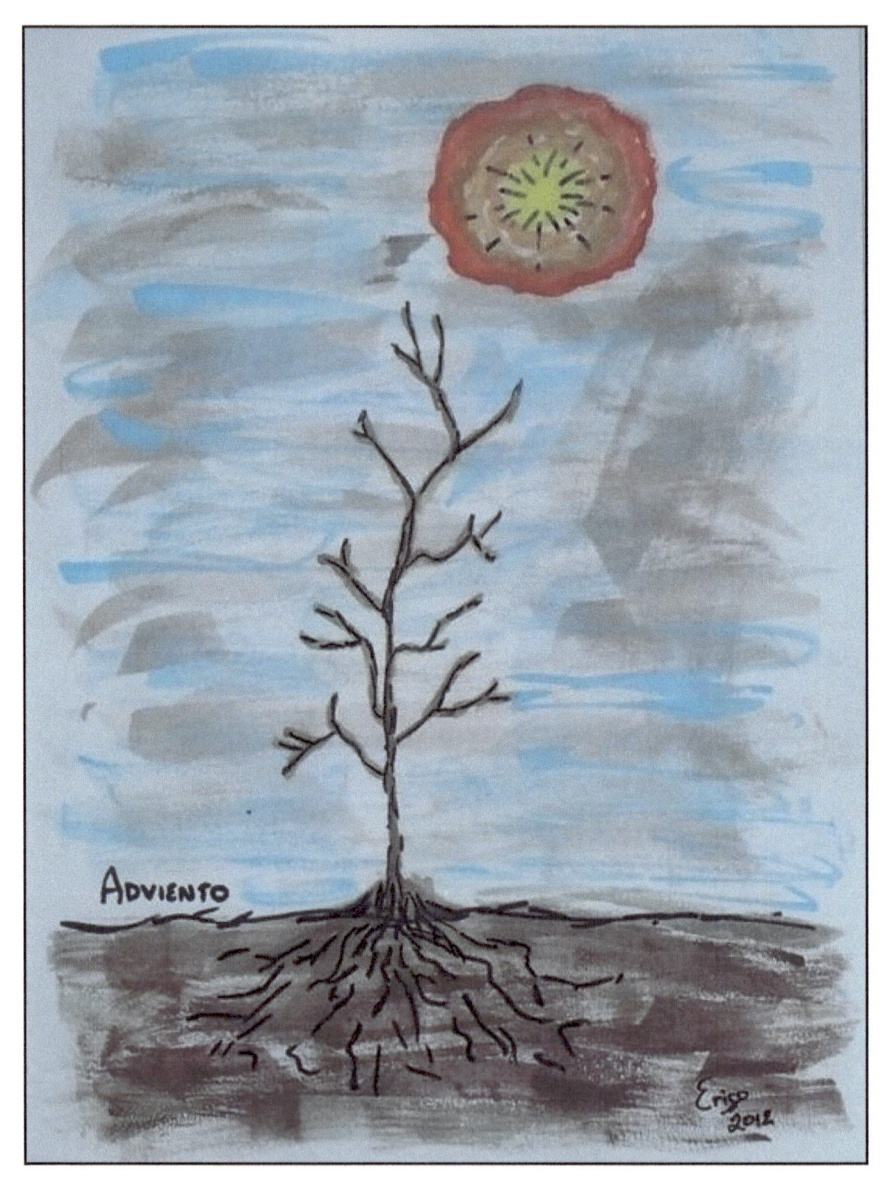

Adviento/Advent
*Watercolor, 2012*

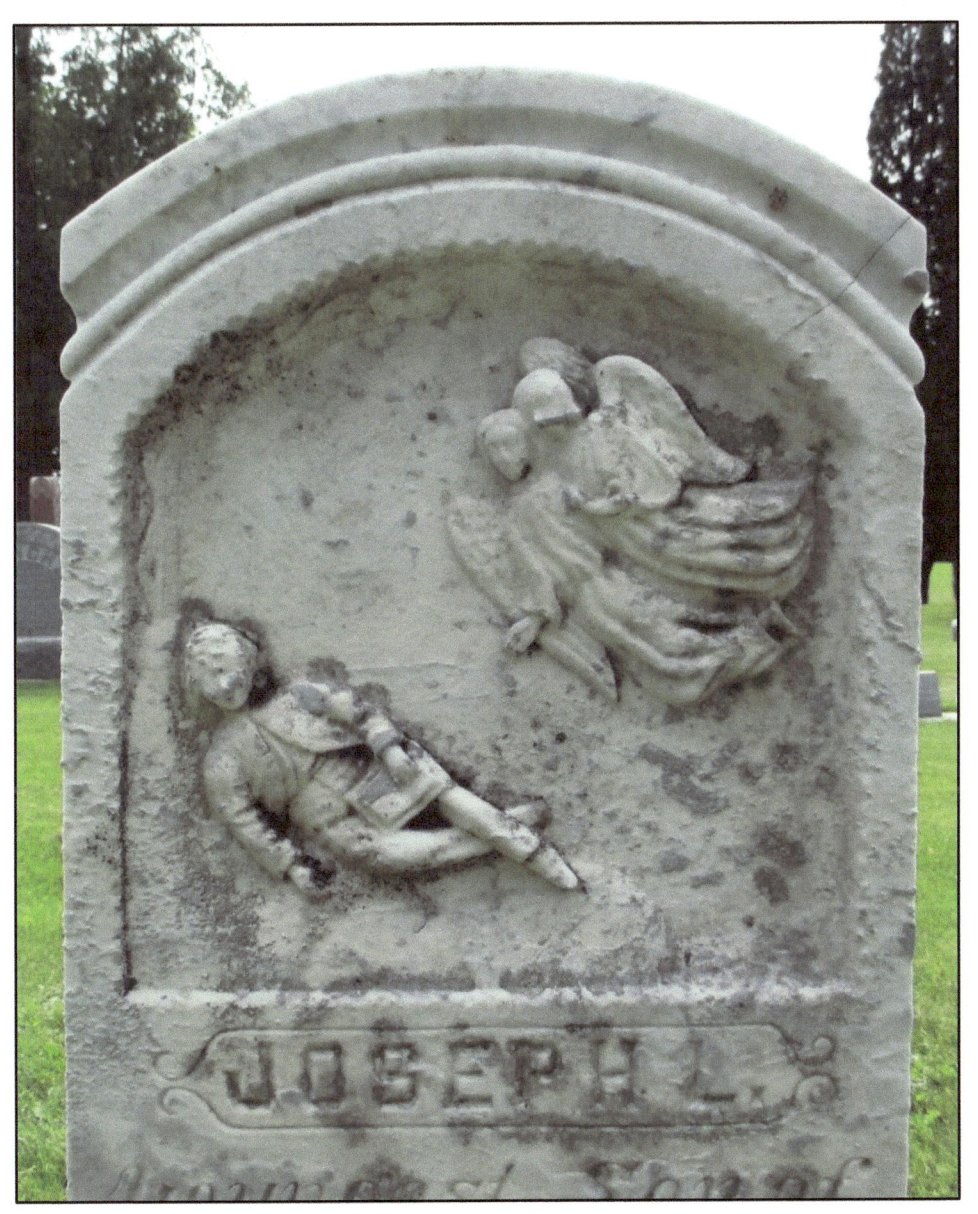

In Angels' Arms

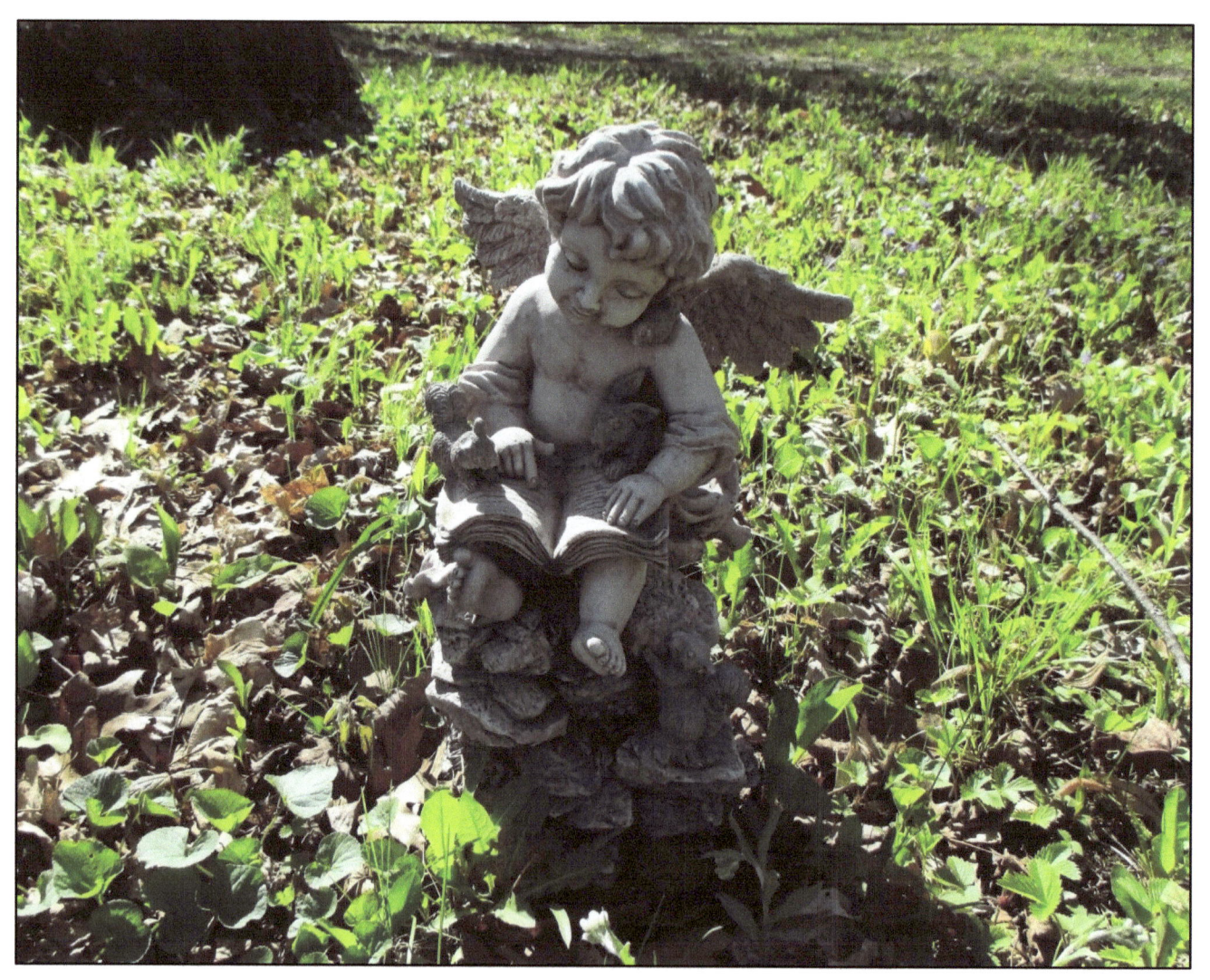

Forest Companions

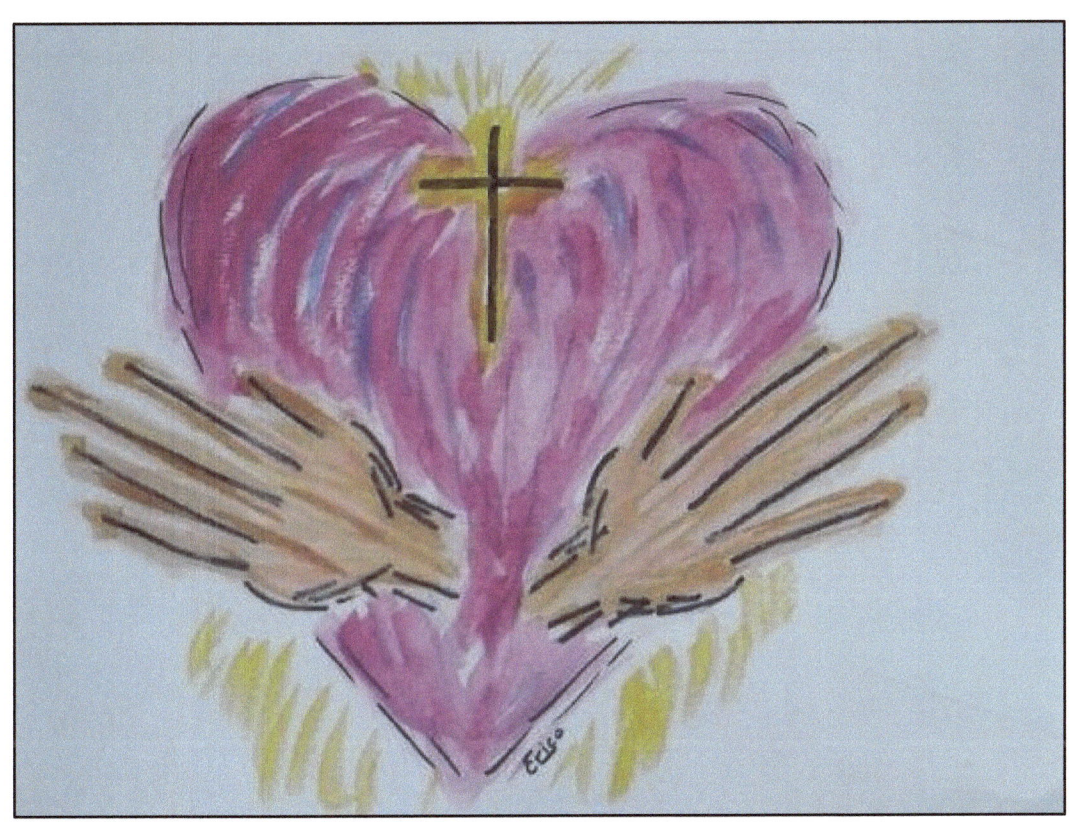

Cross My Heart
*Watercolor, 2012*

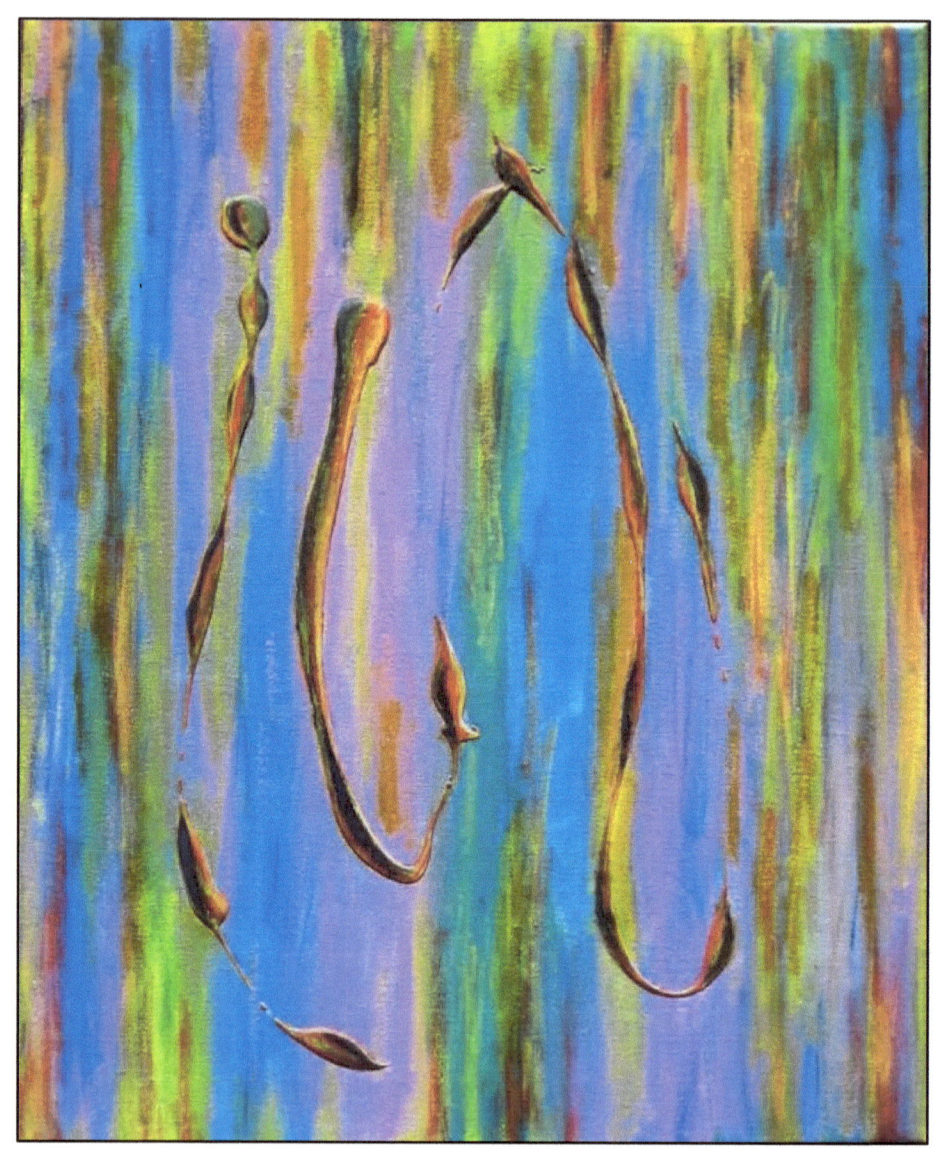

Family
*Acrylic, 2012*

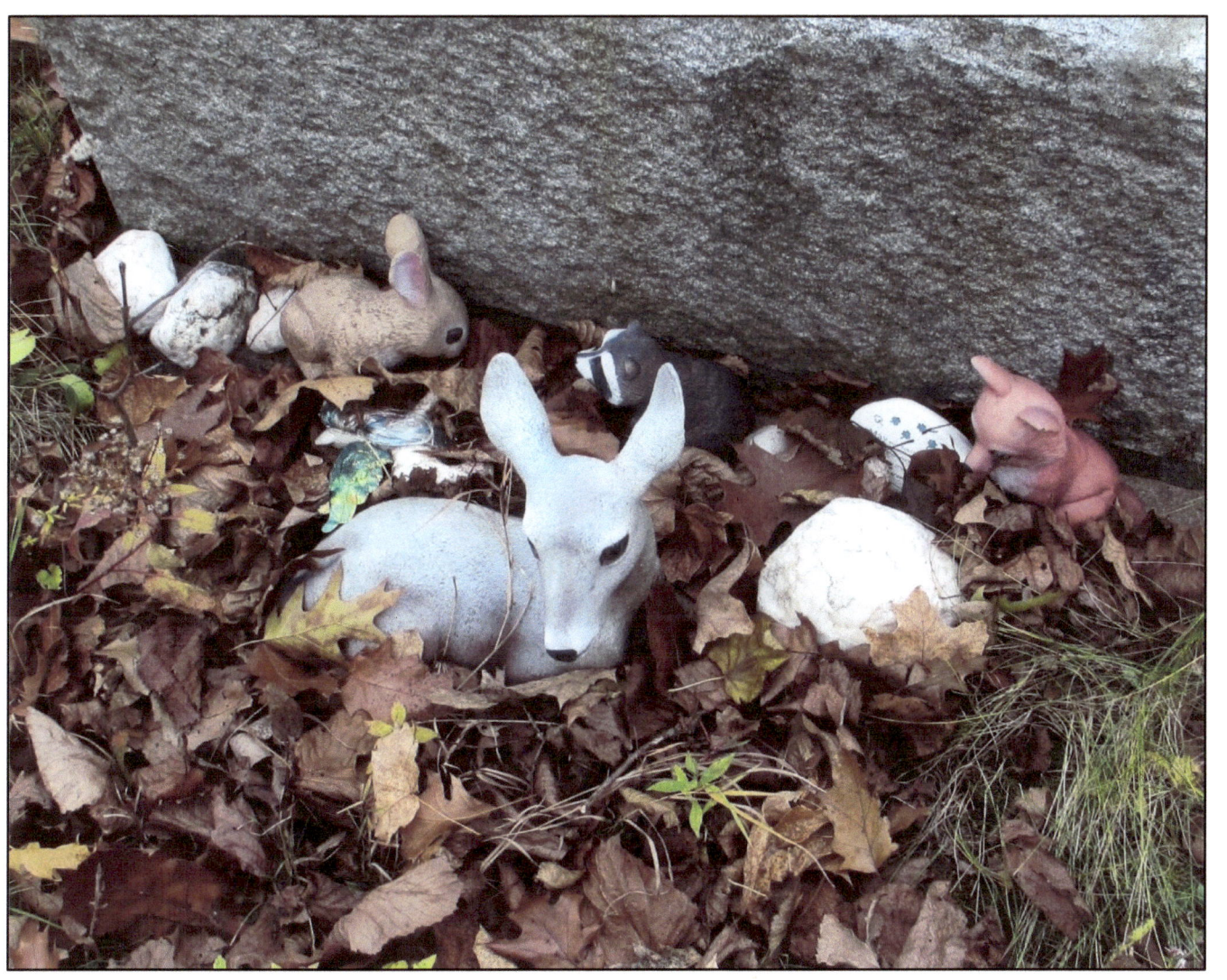

Gather Near

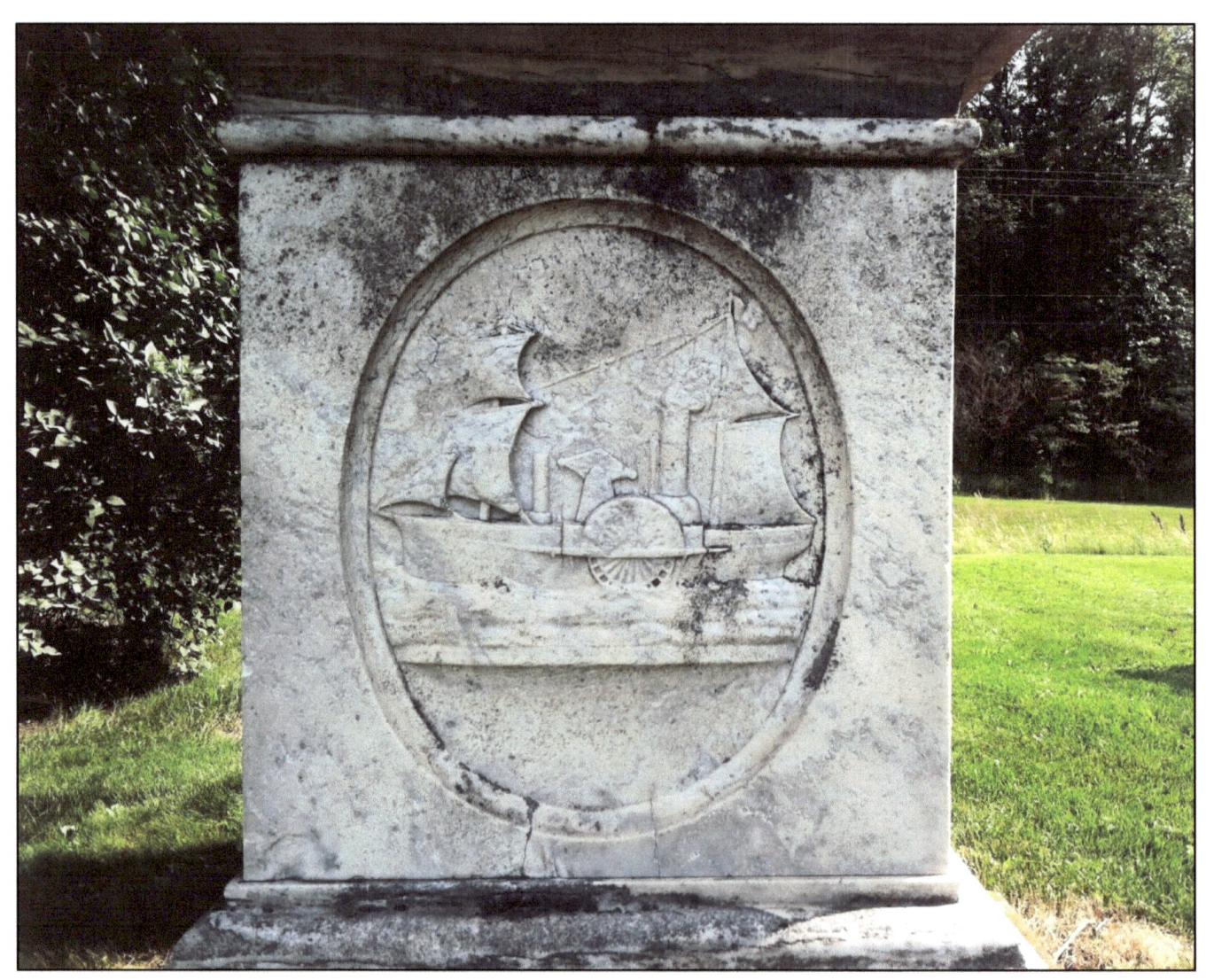

Landlocked

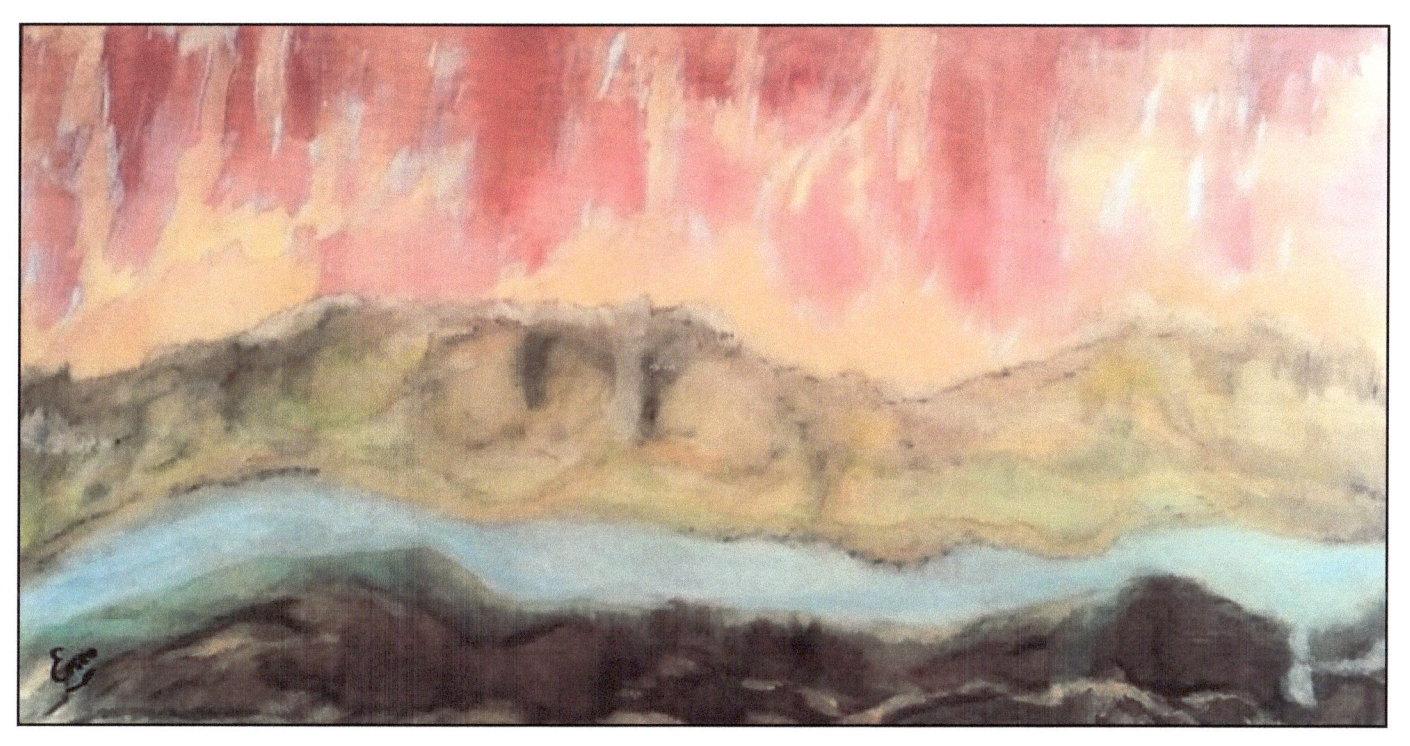

## Mountain View
*Watercolor on wood, 2014*

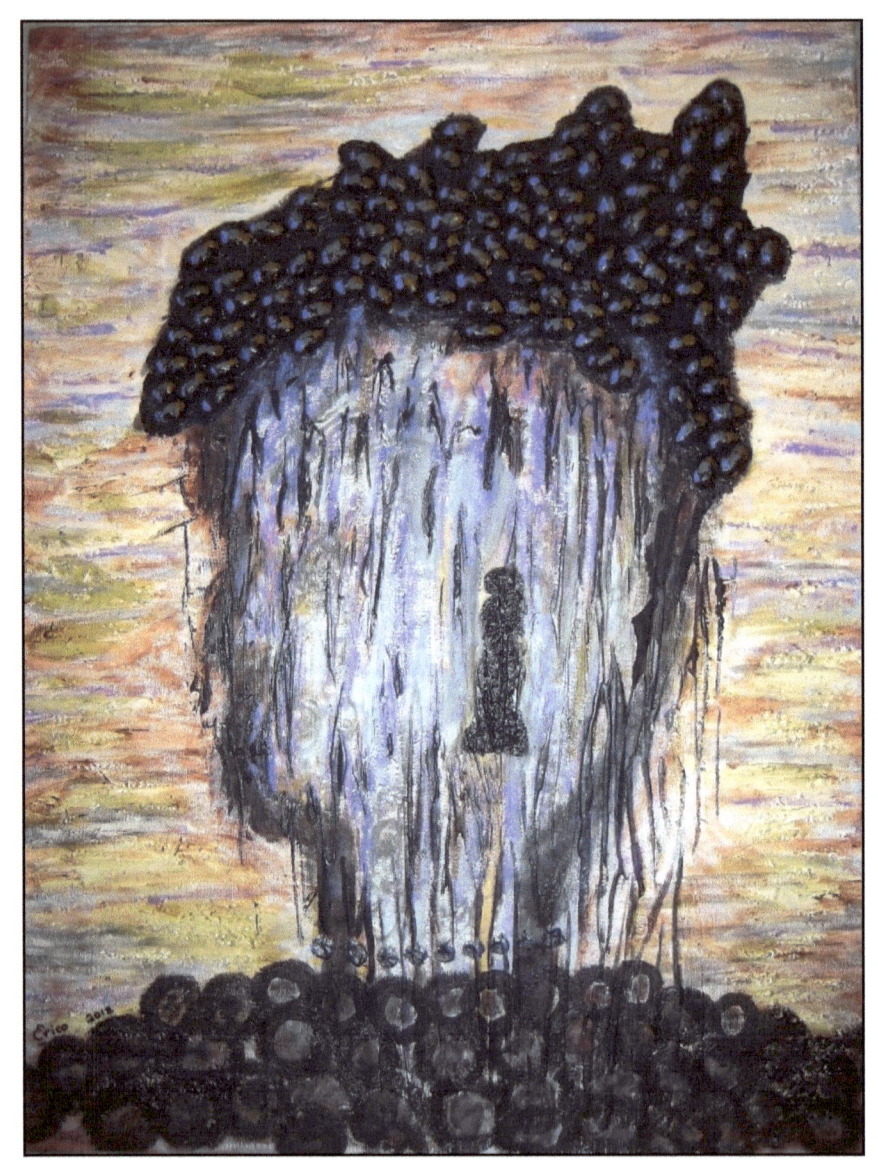

**Fading Beauty**
*Mixed media, 2012*

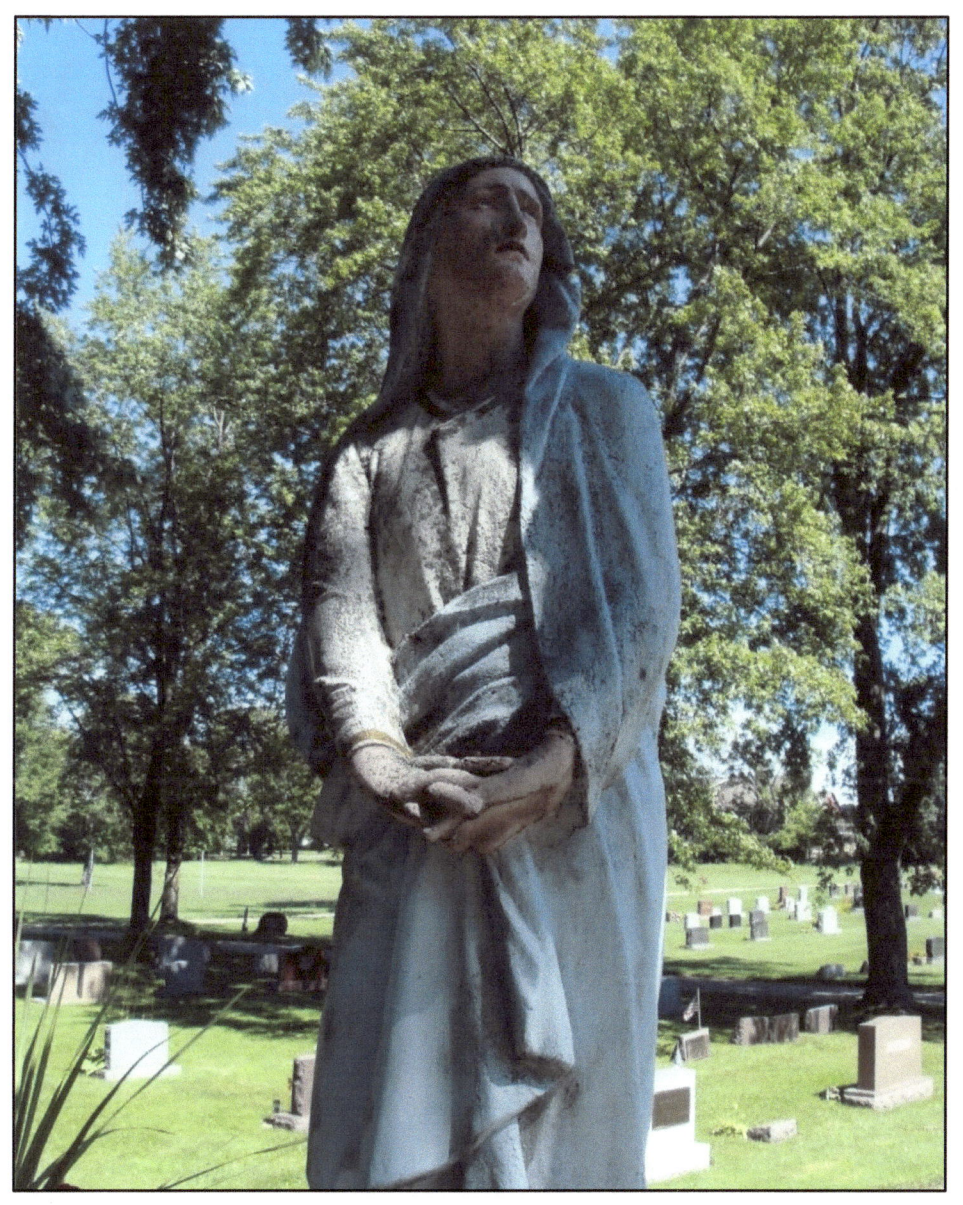

Mother Mary

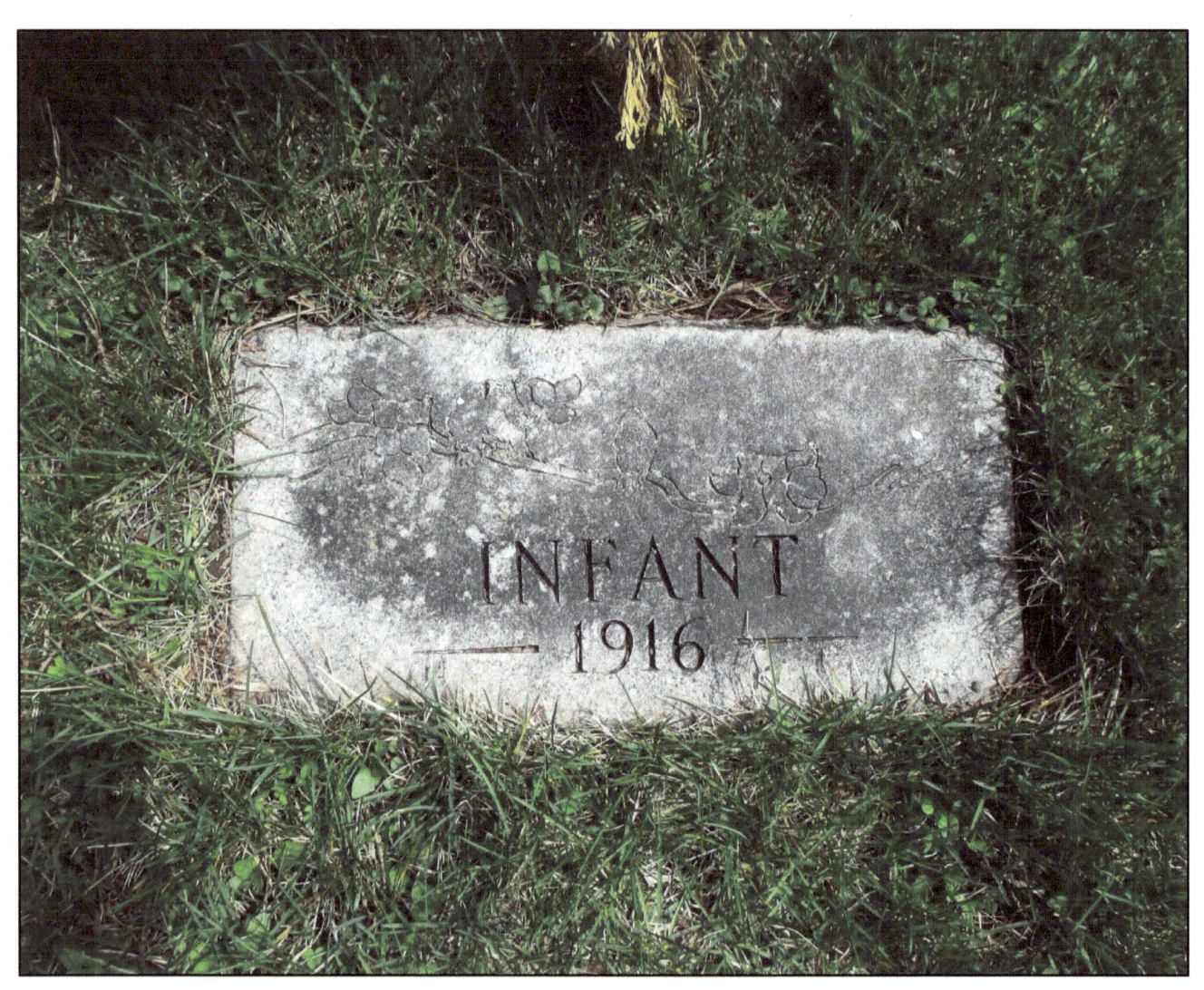

Infant

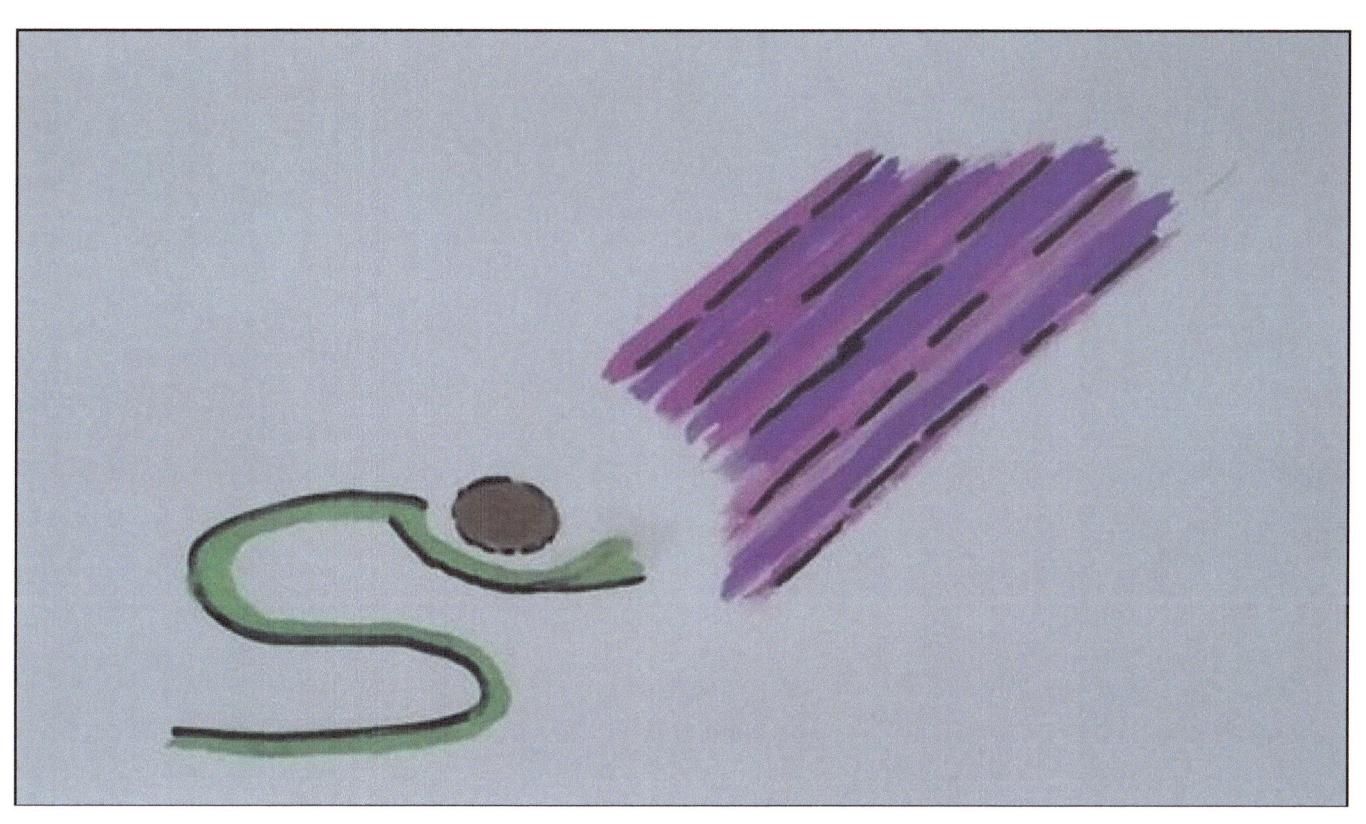

Todo Es Dado/All is Given
*Watercolor, 2012*

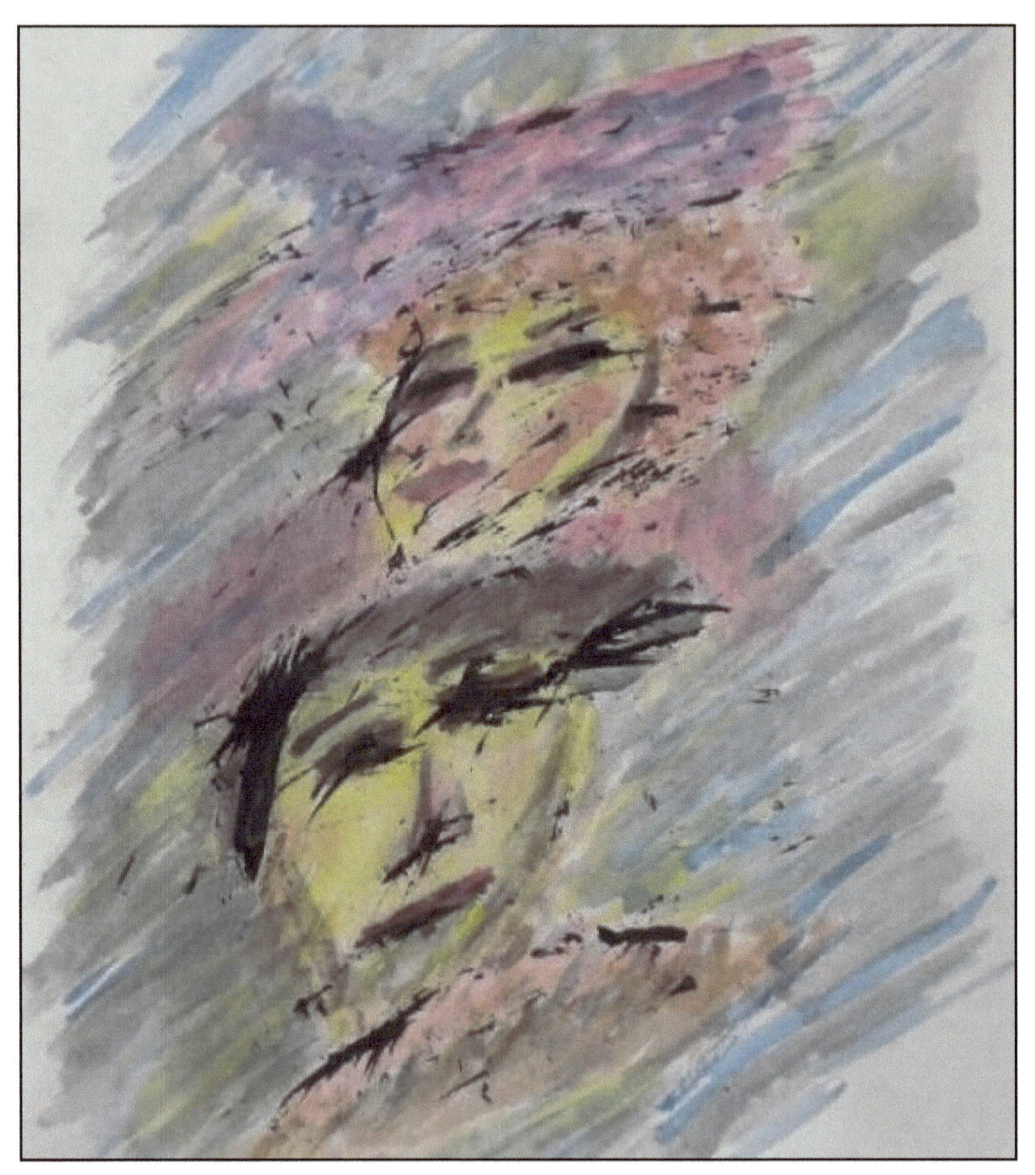

**Windblown**
*Watercolor, 2012*

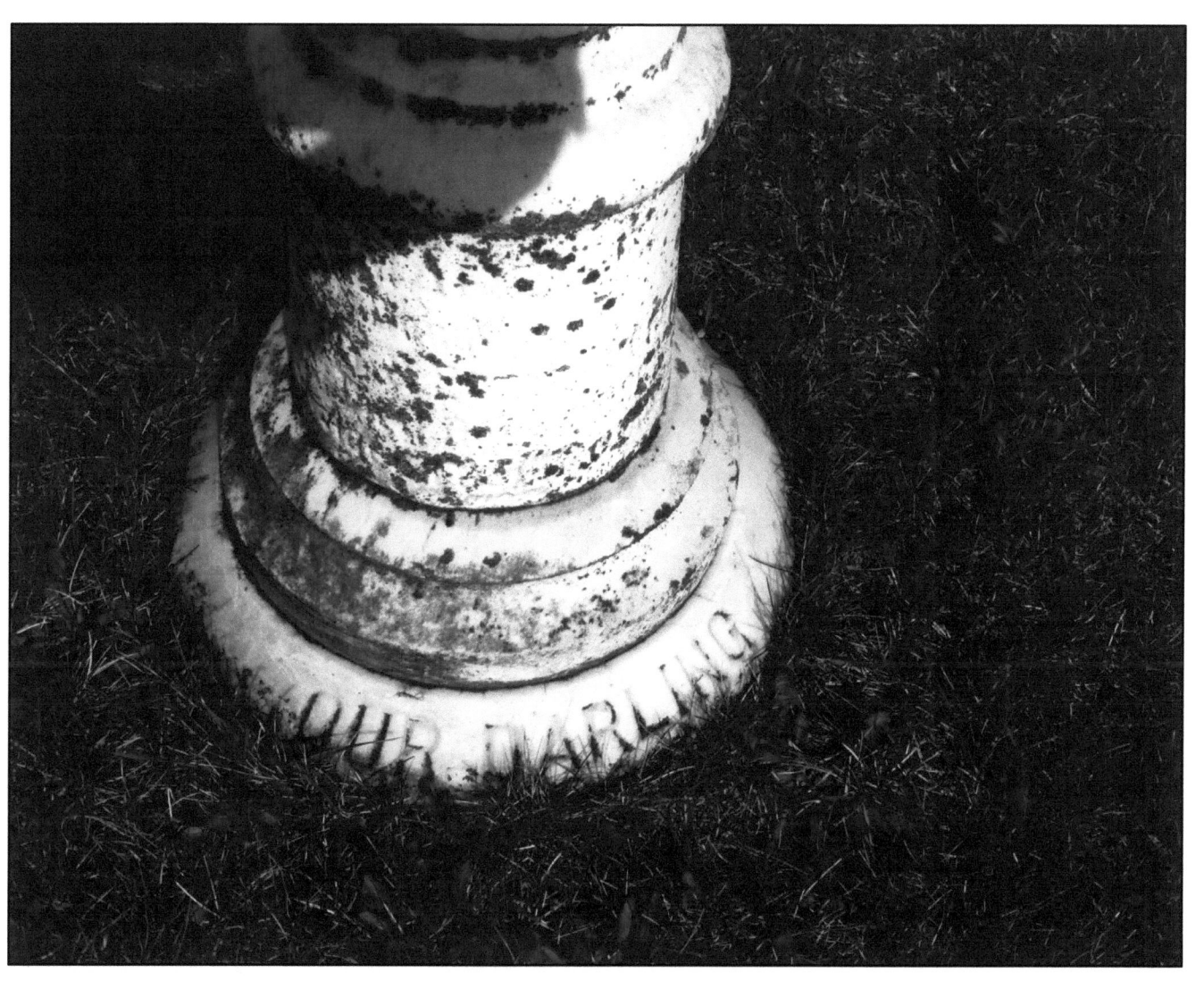

Our Darling

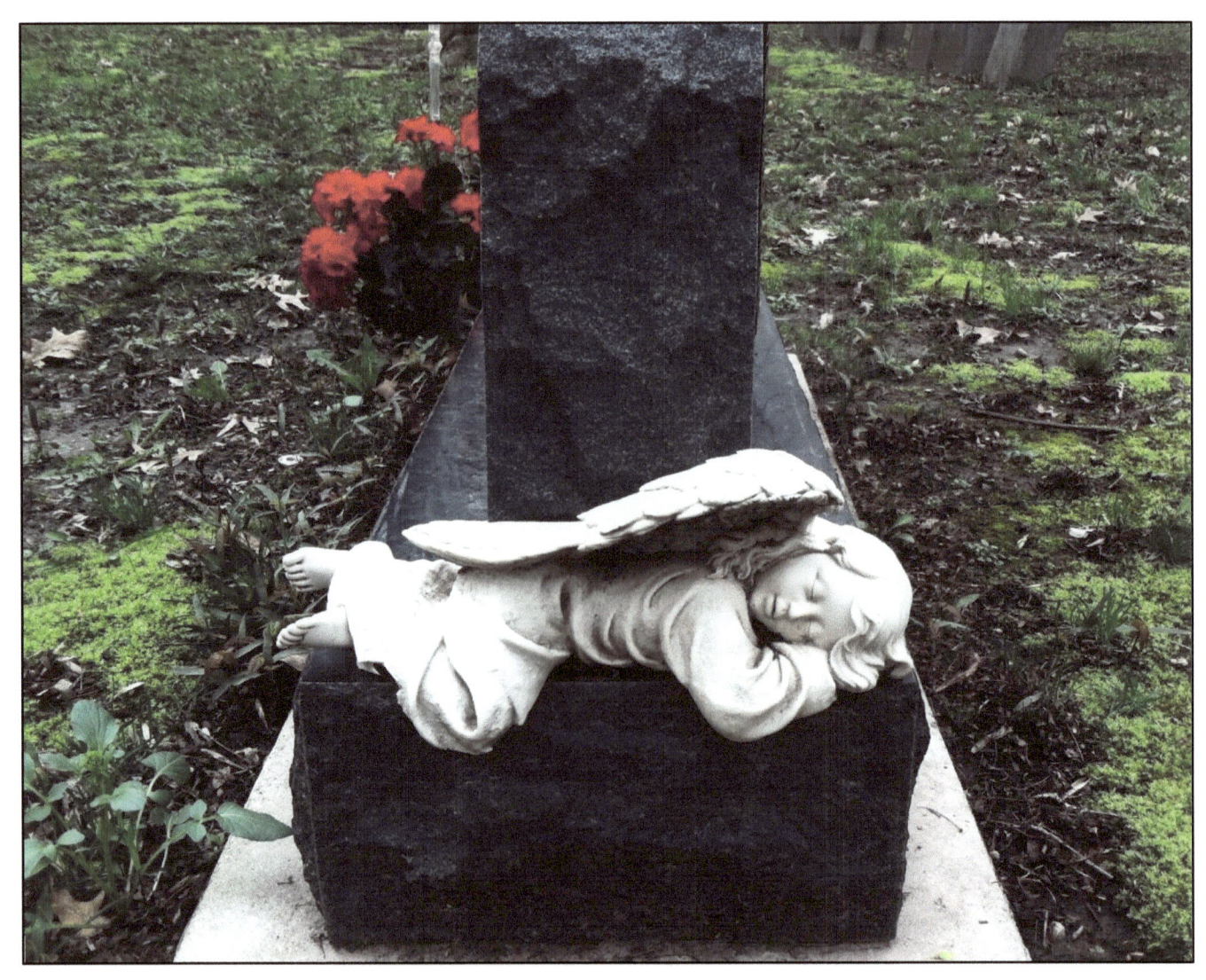

Restful Angel

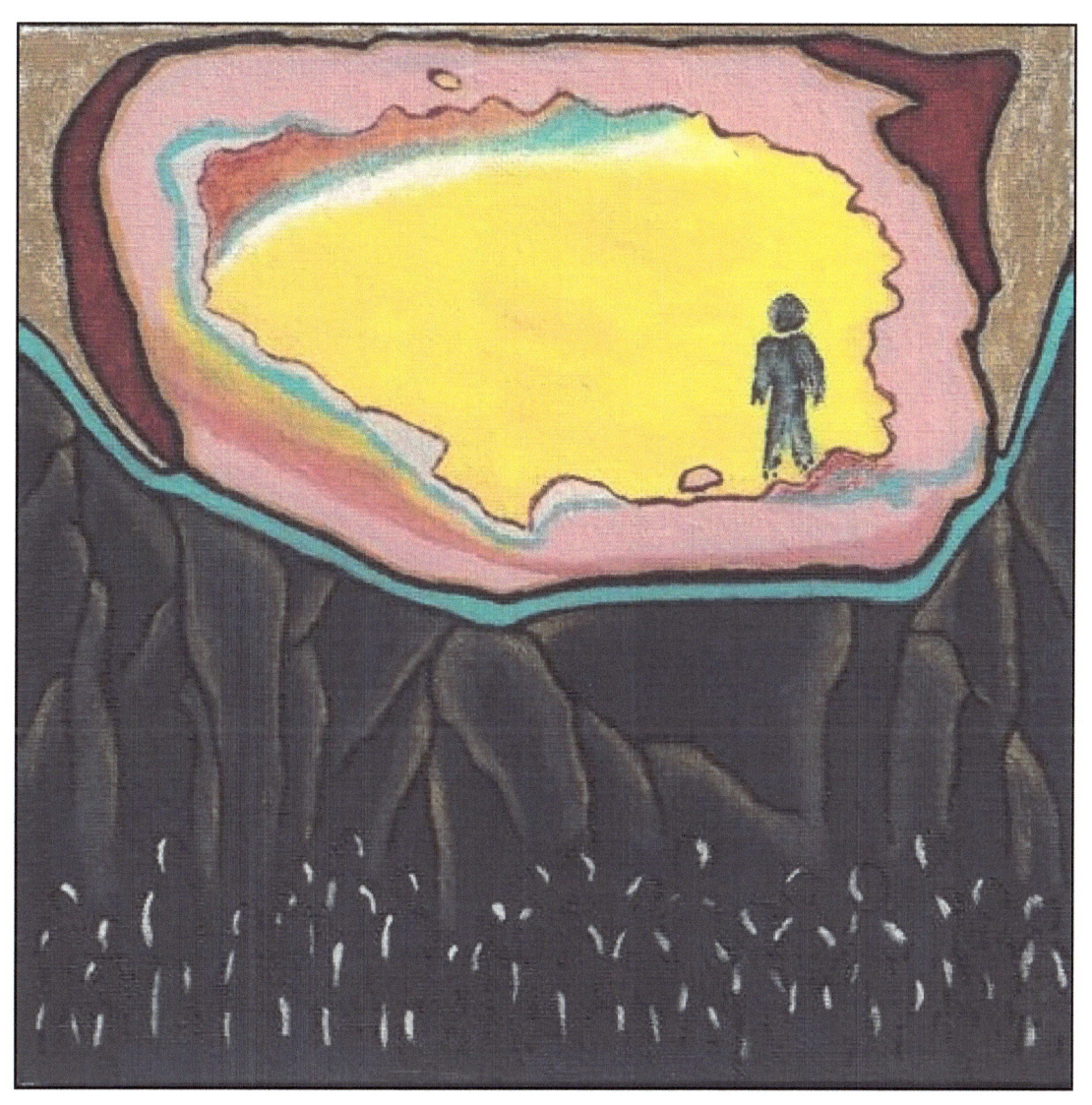

**You Are Not Alone**
*Acrylic, 2013*

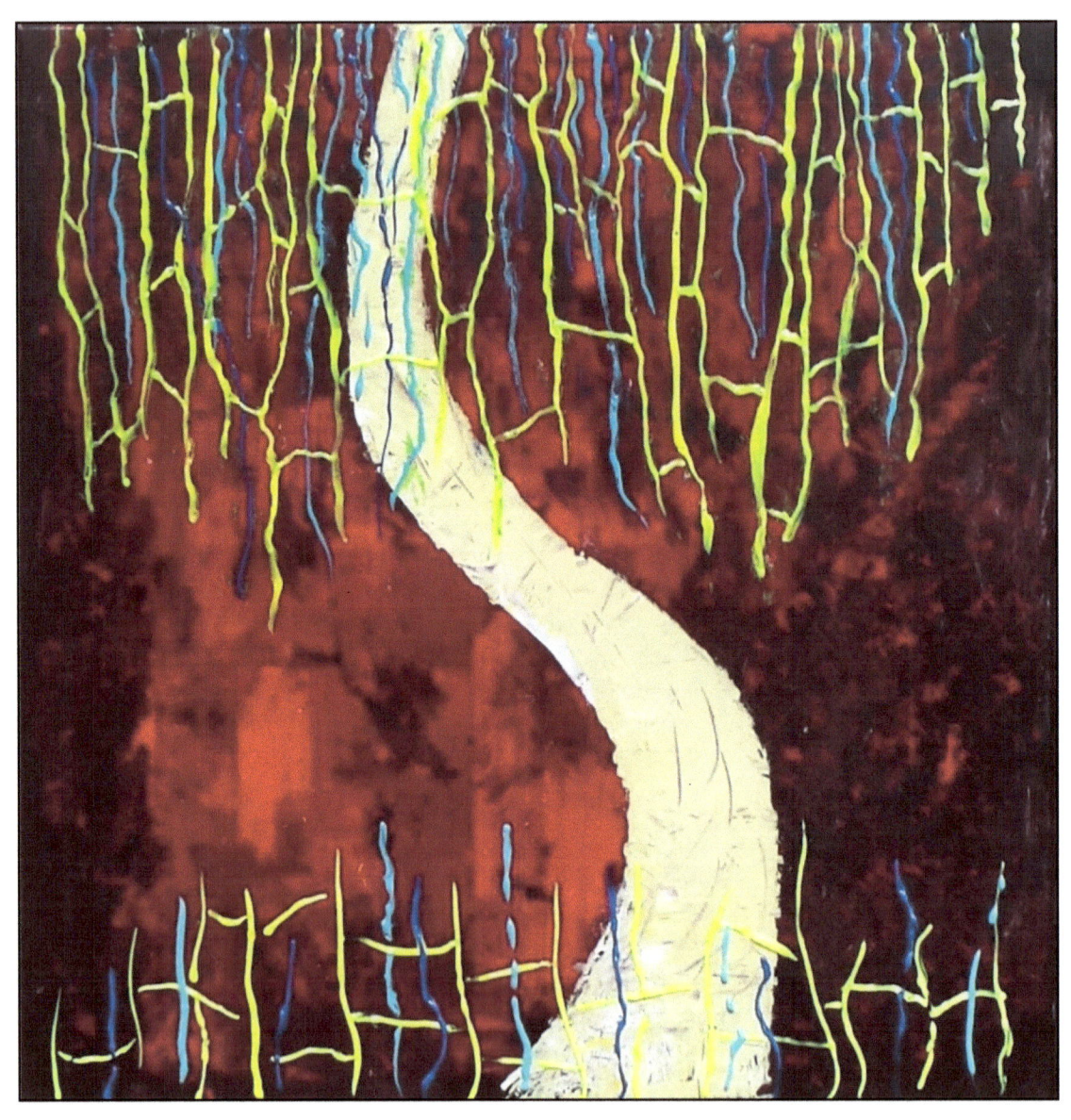

### The Road Is Long…
*Acrylic on wood, 2014*

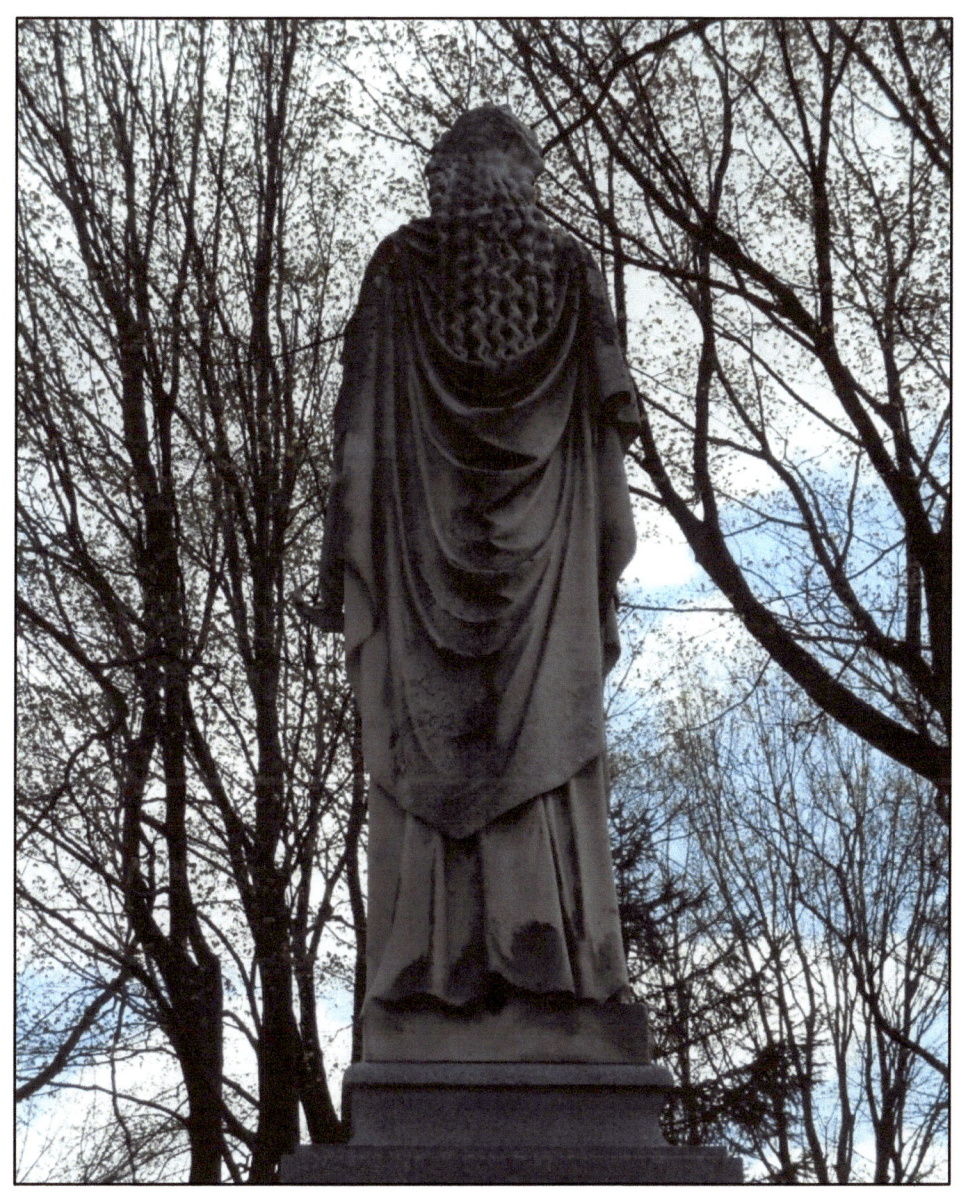

Solitary Path

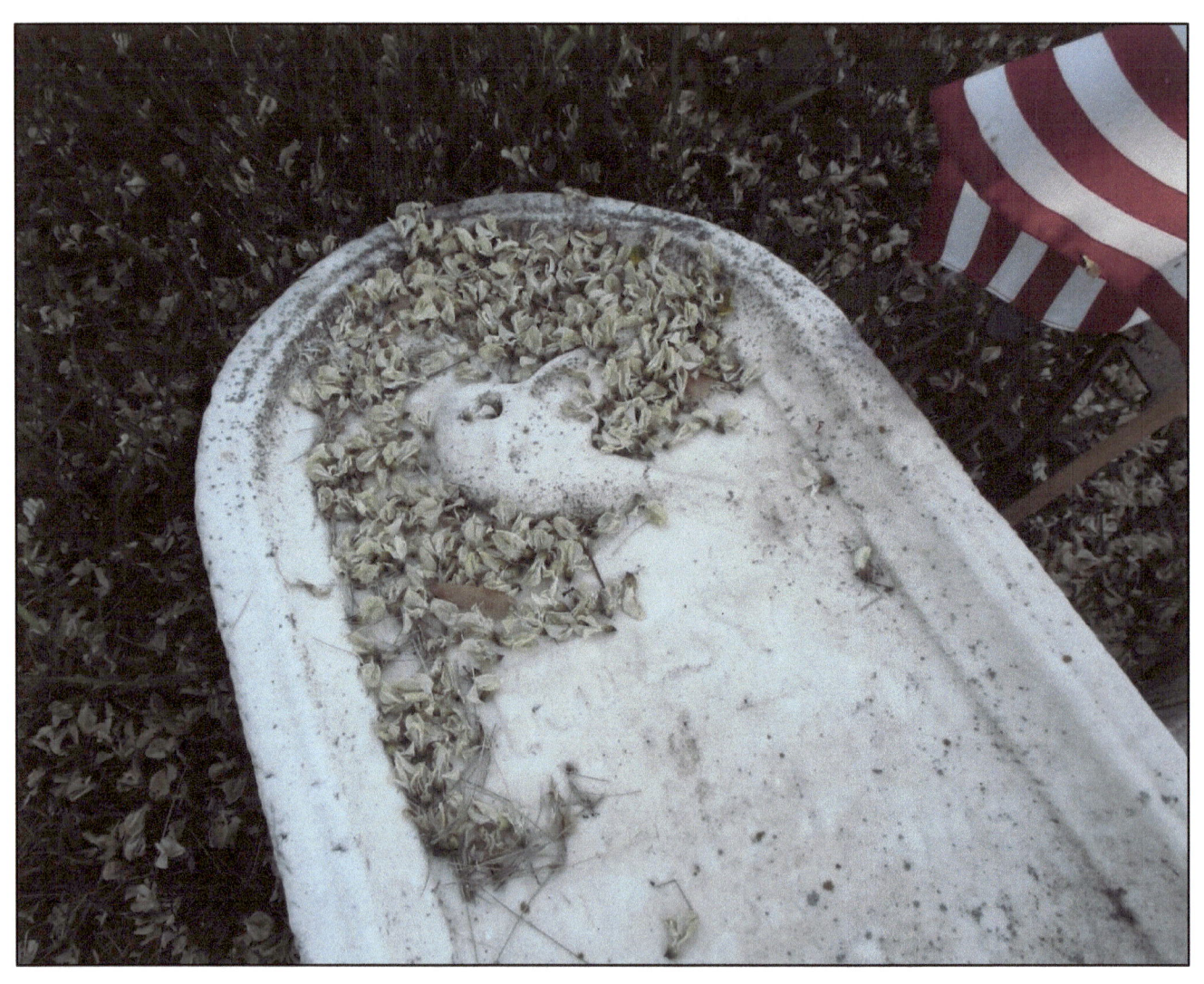

Rest in Flowers

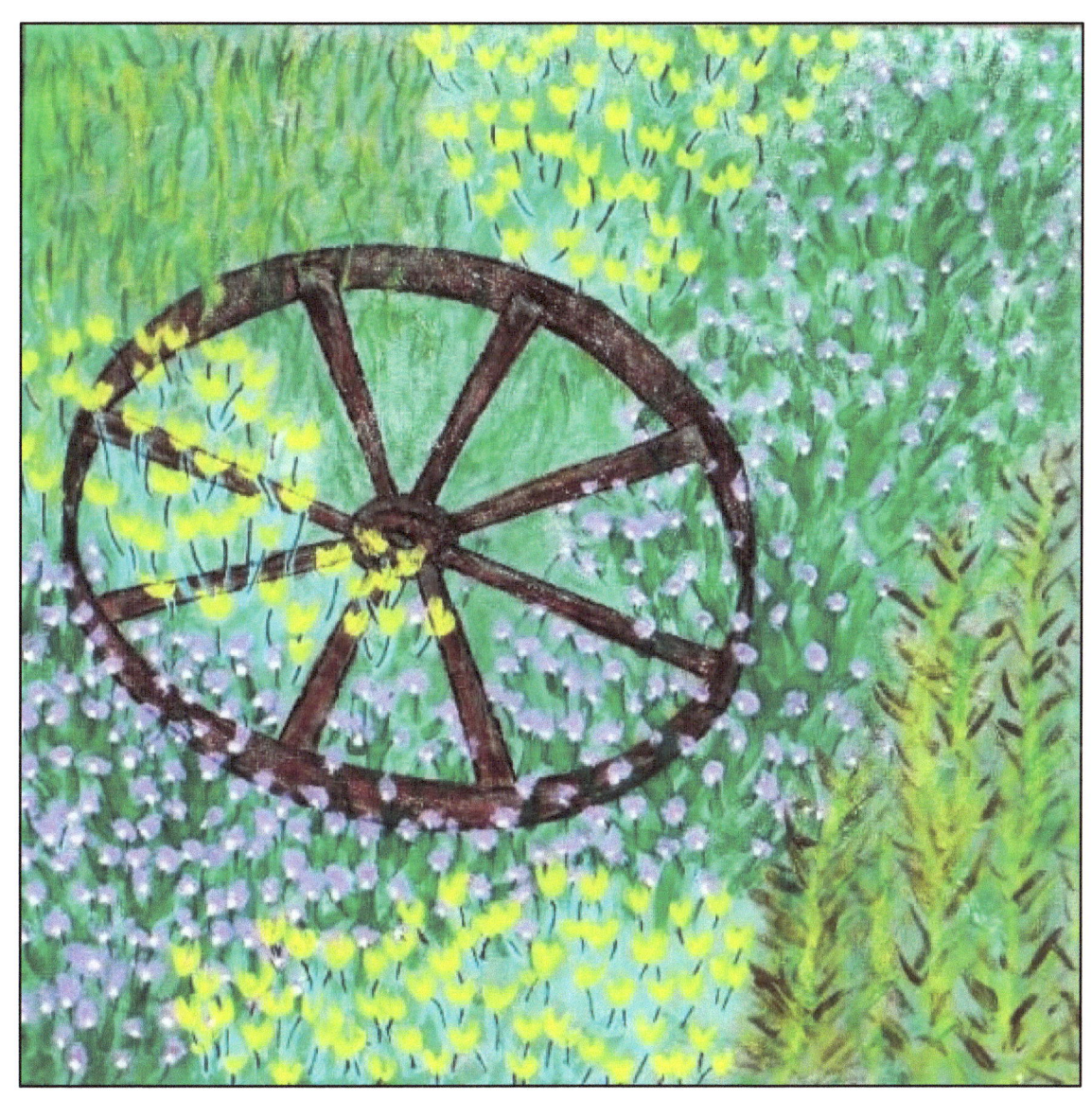

## Wheel of Transparency
*Acrylic, 2012*

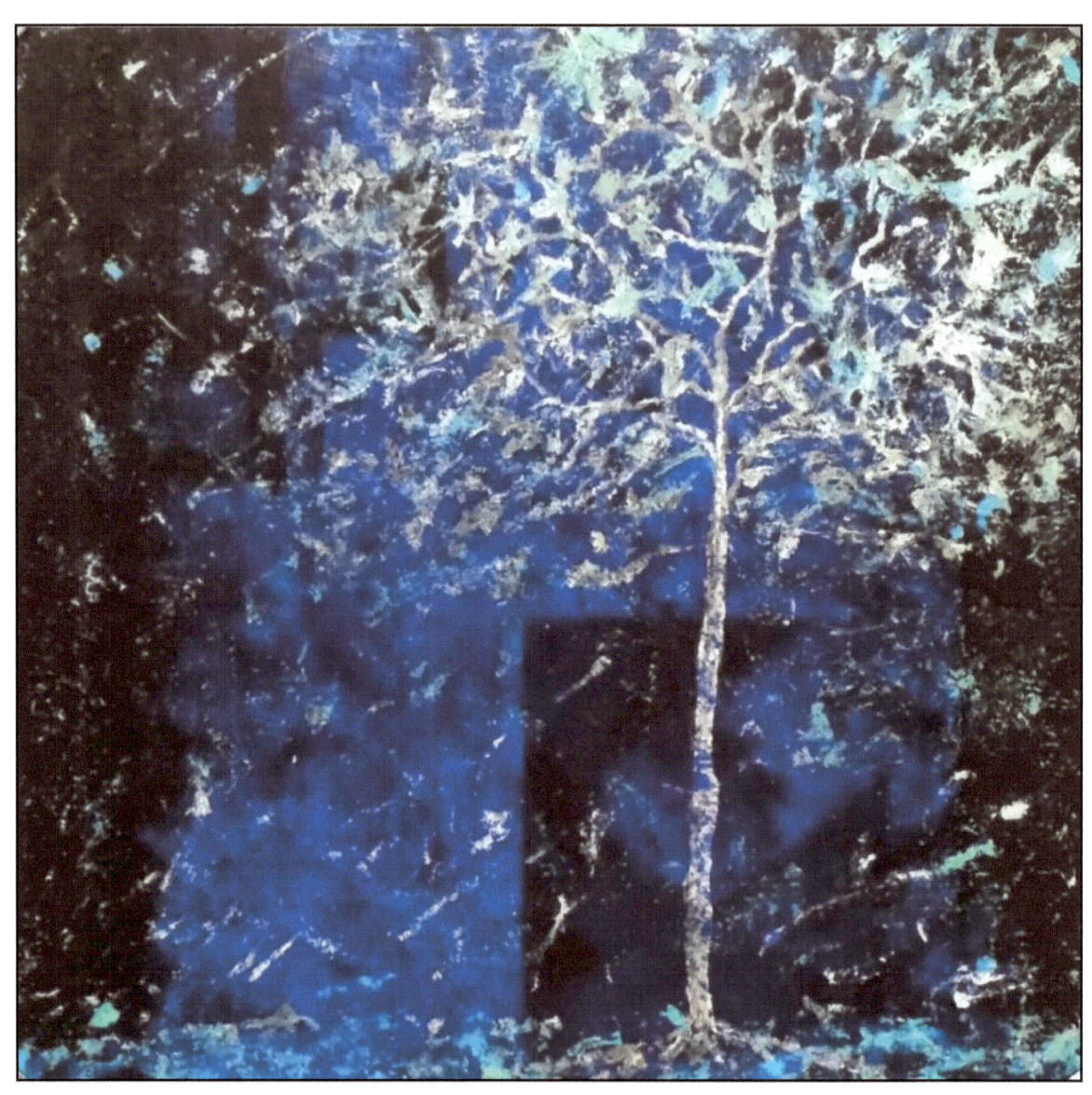

Storm's A-Comin'
*Acrylic on wood, 2014*

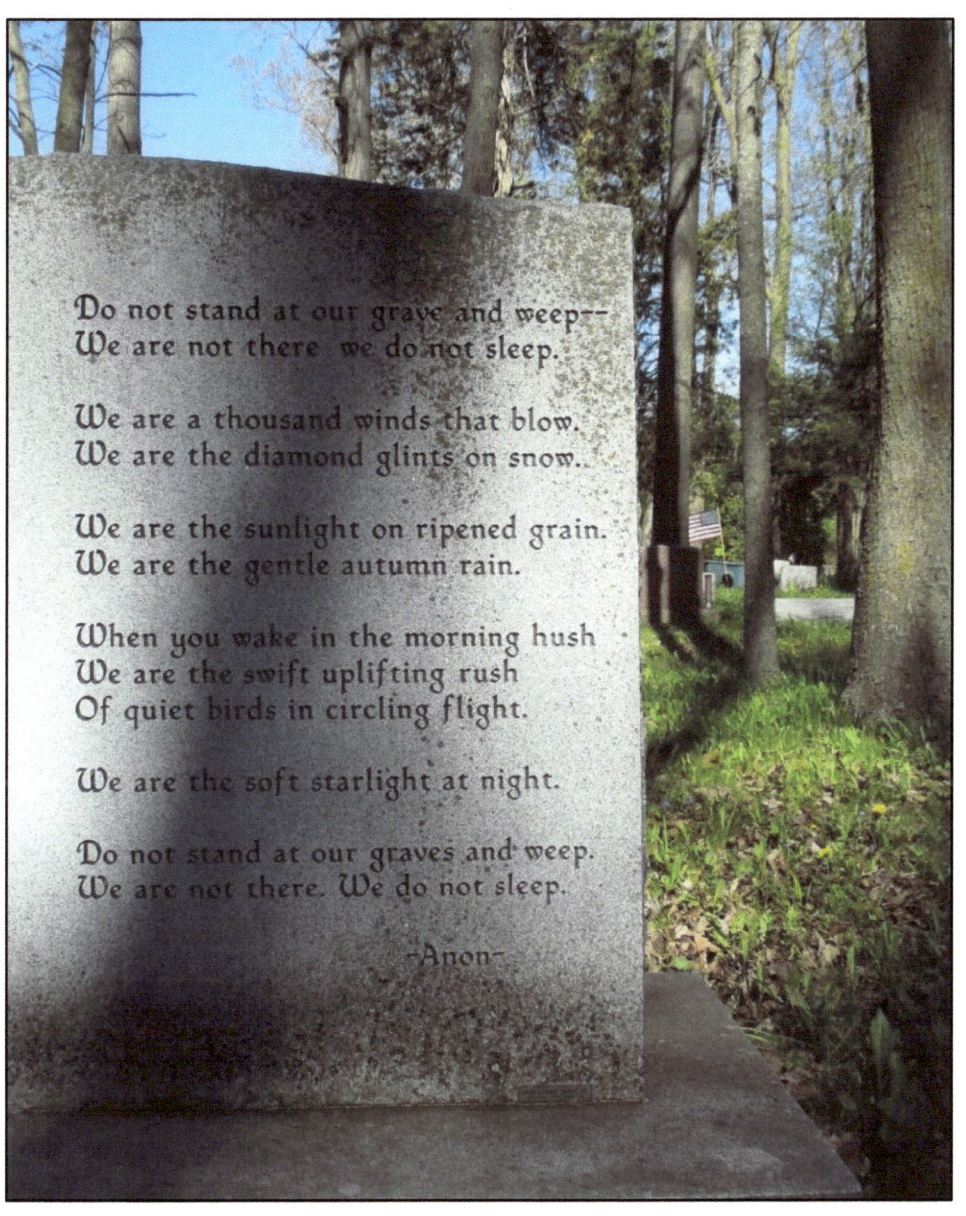

We Do Not Sleep